SYDNEY N.S.W.
23/1/02

A QUESTION OF HONOUR

A QUESTION OF HONOUR

The Life of Lieutenant General Valentine Baker Pasha

by

Anne Baker

LEO COOPER
LONDON

DEDICATION

To the Memory of my dear husband
Valentine Edward Baker
who wrote this book with me and was
my inspiration.

First published in Great Britain in 1996
by
LEO COOPER
190 Shaftesbury Avenue, London WC2H 8JL
an imprint of
Pen & Sword Books Ltd,
47 Church Street,
Barnsley, South Yorkshire S70 2AS

A CIP record for this book is available from the British Library

ISBN 0 85052 496 2

Typeset in 10/12½ pt Plantin by Acorn Bookwork, Salisbury, Wilts
Printed in Great Britain by Redwood Books, Trowbridge, Wilts

ACKNOWLEDGEMENTS

My grateful thanks are due to:

Sir Robert Mackworth Young for permission to read at the Queen's Library, Windsor Castle, and for the gracious permission of Her Majesty the Queen to publish letters from the Queen's Library.

Miss Jane Langton, Registrar of the Royal Archives, Windsor Castle.

The late Sir Ronald Wingate, Bart, CB CIE, OBE for his great encouragement.

Mr. Simpson of the Royal Commonwealth Society, for help and advice.

The Royal United Services Institute for the loan of books.

Lt. Col. P.K. Upton and Major P.D. Wheyman Meakins of the Home Headquarters, the Royal Hussars (PWO), for helpful advice and the loan of the History of the Regiment.

The National Army Museum, Chelsea for photographs and background material.

Captain Patrick Stewart, late 12th Lancers, and author of the History of the Regiment, for help and advice.

The University of Durham School of Oriental Studies, for permission to publish extracts from the Diary of Sir Reginald Wingate.

The University of Sheffield for Sir Samuel Baker's correspondence with Lord Wharncliffe.

Mr. Pinecoffin and the Staff of the British Museum.

The Staff of the Public Relations Record Office.

The late Robin Baily CBE for his invaluable 'Memoirs'.

The late Miss Helen Mills for the kind gift of family letters and photographs.

Mr. Roger Elliott for his excellent photography.

Gillian Baker for her invaluable help and for the typescript of the book and, lastly, all those friends who so kindly helped me and who are too numerous to mention here.

January 1995   **Anne Baker**

SOURCES

Letters read by gracious permission of Her Majesty the Queen at the Queen's Library, Windsor Castle.
Original letters from General Gordon to Sir Samuel Baker and letters from Colonel Valentine Baker and other members of the family.
The British Cavalry by Colonel Valentine Baker.
Clouds in the East by Colonel Valentine Baker.
War in Bulgaria by Colonel Valentine Baker.
Ismailia by Sir Samuel Baker.
Albert Nyanza – Great Basin of the Nile by Sir Samuel Baker.
Eight Years Wandering in Ceylon by Sir Samuel Baker.
With Rifle and Hound in Ceylon by Sir Samuel Baker.
A History of The British Cavalry Volumes I and II by Lord Anglesey.
Ich Dien! Memoirs of the 10th Hussars by Lt. Col. R.S. Liddle (pub. 1895).
The History of the Twelfth Lancers by Captain Patrick Stewart.
Baker of the Nile by Dorothy Middleton.
Sir Samuel Baker, a Memoir by A. Silva White and Douglas Murray (1895).
The Tenth Royal Hussars by Michael Brander.
The Model Major General by Joseph Lehmann.
The Reason Why by Cecil Woodham Smith.
The True Blue by Michael Alexander.
Turkey in Europe by James Baker.
Florence Nightingale by Elspeth Huxley.
Florence Nightingale by Cecil Woodham Smith.
Bismark by Richard Kisch.
The Life of Benjamin Disraeli by George Earle Buckle.
The Life of Robert, Marquis of Salisbury by Lady Gwendolene Cecil.

Edward the Seventh by Philip Magnus.

Queen Alexandra by Georgina Battiscombe.

Queen Victoria by Elizabeth Longford.

The White Nile by Alan Moorhead.

In Relief of Gordon: Lord Wolseley's Campaign Journal of the Khartoum Relief Expedition.

Wellington by Elizabeth Longford.

The Letters of Queen Victoria in three volumes, edited by Arthur Christopher Benson MA, and Viscount Esher, GCVO, KCB (pub. 1908).

The Youthful Queen Victoria by Dorma Creston.

Queen Victoria and her Prime Ministers by Algernon Cecil.

The Age of Elegance by Sir Arthur Bryant.

Wingate of the Sudan by the late Sir Ronald Wingate, Bart.

The Journals of Major General Gordon at Khartoum – printed from the original MSS by A. Egremont Hake.

Extracts from the Diary of Sir Reginald Wingate.

Original report by Lord Dufferin (1882) on Egypt.

Also many hitherto unpublished letters and correspondence.

CONTENTS

PREFACE

Few people now remember the scandal which rocked the breakfast tables of so many respectable citizens on the morning of 3 August 1875 – few people remember, but, even now, an occasional article appears in one of the papers, and we see again in our imagination, the red-plush seats of the old-fashioned railway carriage – still made as much like an elegant horse-drawn carriage as possible, with its high step, its swinging lamps, its elegant cord binding to the cushions, and the beautifully upholstered and buttoned seats. We see the tall dashing soldier, a Colonel, late of the 10th Hussars, sitting opposite the vivacious and attractive young lady who was already seated in the compartment when he stepped into it at Liphook Station, her trunk or 'box' tightly strapped beside her, her bonnet beribboned, her hands in cotton gloves. We can almost feel her excitement at starting on her holiday journey to Switzerland, and escaping from her country home on this fine hot May day. But afterwards, we can only recall the horror of that same young lady, screaming for help, hanging to the door, standing upon the running-board supported only by the strong arm of Colonel Valentine Baker – how the train swayed to a halt, and how from that day the Colonel was to suffer terrible humiliation, disgrace and misery. How from that ten minute journey from Woking to Esher, he was to pay all his life, to lose all that had made his life worth living – honour, distinction in his Regiment, and the appreciation of the Queen.

Very few articles, however, describe the character of the Colonel, his gentleness, his kindness and thoughtfulness, his love of horses – very few know of the far-reaching reforms which he brought to his regiment, reforms which were later almost all adopted by the whole Cavalry – or his introduction of a much swifter form of drill; his dauntless gallantry in the Kaffir and Crimean Wars – or how determinedly and successfully he fought back for his reputation after the 'incident'. Few people recall his brilliant command of the Turkish Forces at Tashkessan when he rescued a whole army, or his brave attempt, when in Egypt, to save the beleaguered garrisons of Sinkat and Tokar when attacked by the followers of the Mahdi. They do not know of the faithful trust which the Prince of Wales always put in him.

He seemed to possess the outstanding powers of organisation which belonged equally to his elder brother, Sir Samuel Baker, and a devotion to his Queen and country which could survive disgrace, banishment, privation, and, finally, perhaps, a broken heart.

★   ★   ★

The British Cavalry and its development was the consuming interest of Valentine Baker's life and so his story is necessarily presented in that light. Some of the phraseology used is that of the cavalry of his day. In particular, the word 'Colonel' was used to describe the Commanding Officer of a regiment although his actual rank in the Army was Lieutenant Colonel. Unless this is understood, some confusion may arise in the reader's mind.

A REPUTATION
TARNISHED

1

THE BAKER BROTHERS

Valentine Baker was born on 1 April 1827, the third surviving son of wealthy and considerate parents. His father, Samuel Baker, was a great man of affairs, often travelling to London on business – the owner of a fleet of merchantmen that sailed to every corner of the world – and who was later to become a Director of the Great Western Railway and Chairman of the Gloucester Bank. Although born at his mother's home, Ridgeway Gates, at Enfield, the family moved to Highnam Court, near Gloucester, when Valentine was only six years old, and it was here that he spent his childhood.

It was a beautiful old house, rented from Sir John Guise, built in the time of Queen Anne, with long windows, and a terrace from which the children could scatter on their ponies to ride over the lovely park and into the woods beyond. There were stables and a harness room, horses to be fed and tended, dogs and animals to be cared for. The boys all went to Gloucester Grammar School but their happiest times were in the fields and meadows round the house. There was a certain independence among them and a physical strength which must have been inherited – perhaps from their dashing grandfather, a Naval Captain, who had taken out 'letters of Marque' and in his small ship of sixteen guns, the *Caesar* (formerly called the *Black Joke*), had fought a gallant action against a French frigate of twenty-two guns in 1782 – forcing her to strike her flag. For that action the merchantmen of Bristol presented the Captain with a silver vase, and an oil painting of the encounter.

Samuel Baker, their father, had also struggled for survival in his childhood, for he had been sent to sea when only fourteen years old, so hardship and suffering were not unknown to him. He would have watched with pride, but also with anxiety as his sons grew up with what must have seemed to him rather more than usual physical strength and independence of spirit and with characters which matched his own. The eldest son, Samuel, quite obviously the hero of his younger brothers, was described as 'a strong well-made lad, with a very gentlemanly bearing . . . bright auburn hair and an open, honest countenance.' He was eventually taken away from school and sent to a private tutor who wrote 'It was the dull process of school routine which had discouraged him. During the two years that Samuel Baker was with me, he was more my companion than my pupil. Here he took his gun on the marshes or had a run with a pack of beagles.'

There must have been long discussions at the time as to what would be the best career for the two talented older boys. Sam showed no desire to go into his father's office and he only seemed happy out of doors, with a gun in his hand.

While these weighty problems were being talked over and finally decided upon, the two younger sons of the family, Valentine and James, would slip away without being noticed. Valentine would almost always find his way down to the stables, where, in the dusty harness room, which smelled of oats and home-made saddle soap, he could watch the coachman at work and the stable boys polishing bits and harness for the horses. He would look up to see the various saddles on their stands, reins and bridles and various shining bits all hanging neatly from the walls, and perhaps perch on the wooden stools and trestles to talk to the grooms. It was here that he absorbed, quite naturally, everything to do with his father's horses – the hunting saddles, the bridles and bits for use on the hunting field, and the collar and harness for the carriage in which the coachman, resplendent in top hat and uniform, would drive his mother out to visit her friends in the neighbourhood.

Most of all he would have known every horse in the airy stables, from his father's heaviest hunters to the gallant little pony which he himself rode – he would have known the character and different moods of every one of them – from their lethargy in the hot summer days under the trees in the park, when even to brush the flies away with their long tails seemed an effort, to the trembling enthusiasm created by the sound of a hunting horn in the sharp and frosty days of Autumn.

Meanwhile the three pretty daughters of the neighbouring Parson, the Reverend Charles Martin, whose garden led down to the river dividing the properties, were finding the Baker brothers very amusing and attractive. Henrietta, Eliza and Charlotte were all most talented. Poems and letters still survive in carefully kept albums where drawings of the Vicarage and pressed flowers lie beside Sam's sonnets and Henrietta's and Eliza's paintings of wild flowers. The boys used to pole themselves across the river on a home-made raft for picnics, and the long summer days passed in the most delightful way. They were golden days for the young, but time was rushing on, and soon Sam was sent to Frankfurt to complete his education in Germany. His father, at about this time, decided to give up the lease of their beloved Highnam Court and to buy a much larger and more imposing house of his own.

In 1842 the family moved to Lypiatt Park, in the same county of Gloucestershire, and it was to this new home that Sam returned after his education was completed abroad. A spell in his father's London office proved disastrous – he was obviously quite unsuited to life in London. He was to write later: 'A wandering spirit is in my marrow which forbids rest. The time may come when I shall delight in cities but at present I abhor them. Unhappy the bird in its cage! None but those who value real freedom can appreciate its misery.'

Samuel decided eventually that not only Sam, but his brother John, would benefit by a spell of life abroad, and he arranged for them both to sail to Mauritius to manage an estate there which he had acquired when the island had been ceded to Britain, after the Napoleonic Wars. It was an adventure after the young men's hearts. Their father and mother may well have been surprised when both the young men announced that they were going to get married before the expedition and had decided to take their young wives with them.

Their brides were their childhood companions, Henrietta and Eliza. The young couples were married together on 3 August 1843, in the little parish church at Maisemore, the adjoining parish to their old home, the father of the two girls taking the service. Their little sister Charlotte was a bridesmaid. Soon afterwards the newly-weds set off for Mauritius.

At this time, Valentine and James were still at school in Gloucester. But very soon news of yet another venture arrived from their older brother Sam. The stay in Mauritius had not been entirely a happy one – a baby had died, the island was predominantly French speaking, and there was no shooting or sport for the restless Sam.

Sam's 'wandering spirit' had seized him. He was fascinated by accounts of sport and elephant-hunting in Ceylon and, in 1846, wrote that he had set sail for the island on a reconnoitring expedition. Meanwhile, his wife Henrietta and her sister Eliza were returning home, with his brother John, to prepare to join him.

* * *

It must have been a moment of anxiety to their parents, when their two younger sons, Valentine and James, begged to go abroad with their elder brothers. Young Sam had given such a glowing account of Ceylon that both he and John had decided to emigrate, and to start a real 'family home' on the island.

Valentine, now just twenty-one, was tall and dark. He was possibly the most handsome of the four brothers, and an early picture of him, painted on glass, shows a good-looking young man with arms folded, looking purposefully in front of him. He was hoping to look after the horses on the journey. Samuel Baker decided that his two younger sons could only stay in Ceylon for a year. They should then return to join their regiments – for both were destined for the Army – Valentine was to enter the 10th Hussars, and James the 8th Hussars. They would profit by their experience of the East, and yet both would have a career of their own.

And so, on a mild September day in 1848, Samuel Baker and his wife Mary Ann, watched with heavy hearts as the ship, the SS *Hardwick*, sailed slowly from the docks at Tilbury on the long journey to the Indian Ocean, taking their three dearly loved younger sons with her. The embarkation had been a truly amazing sight, and was described by an eye-witness:–

> Young men and their wives, babies and nurses; the bailiff and his wife and daughter, the groom with the horses, the animals, two of every kind . . . the cackle of poultry, the sad lowing of the cows, the plunging of the bull in mid-air, as he was hauled up: and, last of all, the pack of hounds, scrambling on board over the ship's side.

Their parents had done all that they could to ensure that the adventure would be a success, but it was a sad parting for their fond mother, and perhaps she sensed that she might never see her beloved sons together again. This premonition was well founded. Only two years later, she was to die after a distressing illness. The happy childhood days at Highnam Court and Lypiatt had ended. The four brothers now realised that, together, they would have to face the world without her and the comfort and security of their happy home.

On the voyage, young Valentine attached himself to the groom, Perkes, and made the welfare of the horses his especial care. From their condition on board he made mental notes on the handling of horses on board ship, which were to be of inestimable value to him later in his life.

Although the voyage took about six weeks, it was entirely successful, and on arrival at Colombo the livestock and supplies were landed safely.

There a triumphant young Sam was able to welcome them and transport them to his new settlement at Newara Eliya, where he had chosen to make his home, high among the forests above the sea.

The house, which was almost completed, was long and low, with verandahs and beautiful views of mountains and lakes. It was soon to become a second home for many members of the Baker family. The two pretty young brides were to fill it with their paintings of flowers and their embroidery, and the beautifully carved furniture which they had made specially by local craftsmen. Meanwhile, after various initial setbacks, the farm flourished. Crops were planted and the little estate, which was later to be called Mahagastotte, was to grow in prosperity as the years went by. The fresh mountain air at Newara Eliya contrasted with the tropical heat of the coast, and was ideal for the health of the two young families.

Having helped with the arrival, Valentine lost no time in joining the Ceylon Rifles, determined to fit himself for his future career in the Army. To his elder brother, however, it was the amazing opportunities for hunting and shooting which fascinated him most. Almost at once, Sam began a series of hunting expeditions into the interior, usually on foot, with his favourite hounds from England running beside him. Elephants then had a price on their heads. In great numbers, they would destroy the natives' sparse crops of rice, and rogue elephants from the jungle could cause terrible destruction to the villages. Sam now became a great elephant hunter. He knew the haunts of the herds, he studied their ways and he soon became a brilliant shot, particularly with an enormously powerful elephant gun of his own design.

One such elephant hunt was vividly described by his great friend, Stuart Wortley, afterwards Lord Warncliffe, who travelled out to Ceylon to say with the family in 1851. In spite of the thrill and excitement of the chase, he found that Valentine's loyalty to his new regiment was even then very evident for, against the advice of the whole party, and to the annoyance of his elder brother, he was determined to report back to his regiment 'on time', whatever the temptation to continue in the hunt. Stuart Wortley wrote:

> *19 Nov. 1851.* Samuel Baker shot a fine buck spotted deer at 120 yards, and killed a crocodile. In the evening, party divided . . . Valentine Baker fired at an elephant in the jungle but did not get him . . . The country consisted of small glades, and thick jungle with enormous Banyan, Satin Wood, and Ebony trees in it.

26th . . . Val and I ascended a small hill but saw nothing but endless jungle and magnificent rocky hills covered with forest.

27th . . . went towards Kahalluley, but could not reach it. No coolies up, nothing to eat, and only water to be got after much trouble. No tent up. Slept on our saddles and made a hut with guns.

28th . . . Naturally enough, we awoke hungry. Val being obliged to rejoin his Regiment at Kandy, left us and rode to Badulla, fifty miles, all fasting as he was . . .

The hunt continued without Valentine and the hunters finally secured fifty elephants, but in this small extract from the diary we can see that even at an early age, Val was determinedly loyal to his regiment.

After saying farewell to the happy settlement in Ceylon, Valentine joined his own regiment, the 10th Royal Hussars, in April 1852. He was to spend the next year with them, absorbing their history, tactics and drill, and making lifelong friends among his contemporaries.

2

THE 10TH HUSSARS

Of all the cavalry regiments at that time, the 10th Hussars was perhaps the smartest and had the most distinguished military record. From the Seven Years' War to Battle Honours at Waterloo, the Regiment had gained great distinction in military achievement, and each successive Commanding Officer had added his own particular contribution to their record. It had been a great honour when the Prince of Wales was appointed by the King to be Colonel Commandant of the Regiment in 1793, the Tenth then being designated 'The Prince of Wales' Own Regiment of Light Dragoons'. A year later, '*Ich Dien*' became their motto, and the Prince of Wales' plume with the rising sun their badge.

The name 'Hussars' was borrowed from the Hungarian Cavalry, so much admired in Europe at that time, and it was in 1806 that the Prince of Wales asked his father if the 10th could be clothed and equipped as 'Hussars'. The designation of 'Royal' was bestowed on the Regiment and their name from that date was 'The 10th, the Prince of Wales' Own Royal Regiment of Hussars'.

Dissolute and extravagant though his other companions might be, the Prince took his duties as Colonel of the Regiment very seriously, and very soon the Regiment became one of the smartest as well as the most distinguished in the Army.

Even Beau Brumell, the Prince's friend, was persuaded to join, but he only survived the rigours of a soldier's life for three years. It was said that on the parade ground he always knew his position by the proximity of one red-nosed sergeant. When the sergeant was moved, he completely lost his bearings. On hearing that the Regiment was to be posted to Manchester he gracefully resigned his Commission, saying that 'he was not prepared to go on foreign service.'

Meanwhile, nearly every European state had formed Hussar Regiments, in emulation of the Polish and Hungarian Cavalry at that time, but the 10th was the first regiment in the British Army to be so designated and equipped. It was the first also, to test the new 'Baker' rifle for the Army in 1802, but muskets were more normally carried, even up to the time of the Battle of Waterloo, with the favourite lance, which was described as the 'Queen of Weapons' until the middle of the century.

Their uniforms were magnificent and designed by the Prince of Wales himself. A scarlet cummerbund and a gold braided jacket and pelisse, similar to those of the Hungarian Hussars, gave them an air of great distinction, whilst the accoutrements of the horses on parade were no less remarkable – cowrie shells, split in half, decorated the reins and bridle of the Colonel's horse.*

Later the 10th Hussars were to be known as the 'Shiny Tenth', possibly because of their smartness on parade, but possibly too because, in the South African War, they found it necessary to wear chain mail on their shoulders, to protect them from the cuts of the natives' swords – thus the 'chainy Tenth' was to become later the 'Shiny Tenth'.

A story of the Prince's devotion to the Regiment is told when, in October 1808, they left for Active Service at Corunna. The Prince himself came to see them off, took off his sash and gave it to General Slade, with his jacket and pelisse – a very emotional moment.

Later, when the Regiment covered itself with glory at Waterloo, its deeds were honoured with a silver trumpet, which still hangs in the Officers' Mess, with the inscription:

Purchased
By desire of the
Soldiers of the Tenth or Prince Regent's
Own Royal Hussars
With part of the Prize Money
Arising from the Enemy's Horses
Captured by their Brigade
Under the Command of
Major General Sir Hugh Vivian K.C.B.
At the Battle of
WATERLOO
18th June 1815

---

* As recently as 1965, the Colonel, Prince Henry, Duke of Gloucester, rode a horse with cowrie shells decorating the harness.

It was this inspiring and distinguished Regiment that Valentine joined in 1852. He was a young man already full of ideas on military organisation and concerned with the welfare of men and horses under his command.

At that time, the regiment was stationed at Poona, in India, so the young Cornet had only to travel from Colombo to Bombay to join them. Here he found at once that the exercises and frequent Divisional Field Days provided him with active experience in the field. It was fortunate that General Lord Frederick Fitzalladice was appointed at that time to the Chief Command in the Bombay Presidency, for he was deeply interested in cavalry, as a military arm and particularly interested in outpost duty. The Tenth would be sent off in small parties, many miles into the surrounding country, to bring back rough sketches and reports; it was, perhaps the basis of Valentine Baker's own theory of the 'Light' Cavalry, who should act as 'the eye, the feeler and the feeder of an army'.

After a year with the 10th Hussars, Valentine transferred to the 12th Lancers, a sister regiment, which was about to sail for action against the Kaffirs in South Africa. In those days, under the Purchase System, it was quite usual for transfers to take place when a Regiment was going abroad. Members of other regiments would join, while those who did not want to go could either accept half-pay or transfer.

Valentine was determined to go on active service as soon as possible, he had all the vigour and initiative of his brother, Sam, and longed to travel with his regiment, so that May, 1852 found him sailing with the 12th Lancers towards the Cape to support the Governor, Harry Smith, in the latest, the seventh, war with the Kaffirs.

3

WITH THE 12TH LANCERS

During the early 1840s, war with the Kaffirs had been succeeded by an uneasy peace. However, in 1846 the Chief, Sandile, supported by his witch-doctor, Umlavjeni, organised an insurrection, the situation being worsened by the aggressive attitude of the Basutos to the North, and wandering bands of Hottentots within the colony.

The country between the Fish and Keiskama rivers had already been subject to constant raids, and the Kaffirs had only just retreated to the safety of the Kroome Range of hills when the 12th Lancers arrived.

Sir Harry Smith, who was still slight and very active, often spent more than fifteen hours a day in the saddle, although criticism at home had been growing of his inability as Governor to subdue the wayward tribes entirely. His famous ride to relieve Grahamstown, some fifteen years before, in December 1834, was still remembered with awe and admiration, for he had ridden 600 miles in six days to relieve the town. Since that time, Sir Harry had fought in India, and after winning a famous victory, had brought his white horse 'Alliwal' back with him, only to find that the Kaffir war had blazed out again. In 1851 he was at last forced to send for reinforcements. The 12th Lancers were among the regiments that were sent.

The sea-journey held no anxieties for Valentine. Already, with notebook in hand, he was taking down any improvements which he thought essential for the men and horses on board. He noted that over-crowding was detrimental to the horses; and was to write later:

> The treatment of horses on board ship is a point of great importance, and numbers are usually sacrificed to ignorance on this head. Horses, from con-finement and want of exercise, become peculiarly liable to inflammatory action, and high feeding is sure to bring on a disease of some kind.

He was in advance of his time in recommending better ventilation, cleanliness and exercise.

In a book, written later,* he wrote:

> Great attention should be paid to cleanliness: every horse should, if possible, be moved daily, his stall thoroughly cleaned, and himself brushed over lightly. . . . The head should be well cleaned, and the nostrils should be sponged out daily with a little weak vinegar and water. All the horses on board may easily be moved daily, by leaving a spare stall between every twenty horses. Each horse can then be shifted in succession, and his stall well-washed out before the next horse is moved into it. Ventilation is of great importance.

At length, on 2 October 1852, the '*Charlotte*' arrived at Cape Town, and Valentine was delighted to find that he was among those young officers who were able to purchase horses from Sir Harry Smith's own stables. The compact and sturdy 'Cape Horse' which he bought was to become his favourite mount all through the campaign, and was to be taken by him to India and on to the Crimea. He wrote: 'The Cape, is in my opinion, the *beau ideal* of a light Cavalry Horse; strong, compact, hardy and temperate, and bearing the change of any climate without deteriorating. They are not imported to India in any very large numbers. The Cape horse possesses all the good points of an Arab, with much greater size, he is equally hardy and enduring and more sure-footed.'

Meanwhile he was fortunate that his Commanding Officer was to be William Heathcote Tottenham, a brilliant soldier, who was to become a very close friend in later years. It was under Colonel Tottenham and Colonel Eyre that the 12th was sent in the Spring of 1852 to relieve Butterworth and then join in the round-up of cattle in the Little Kei Area.

Valentine was now to have his first experience of active service. While the campaign was entirely successful, he was horrified at the unnecessary hardship and suffering he found among those soldiers whom the 12th Lancers were sent to relieve. He wrote: 'I remember at the Cape, during the Kaffir War, seeing a regiment march into King William's Town. . . . Their uniforms were torn, and their feet sore from the 'Wait-a-bit' thorns'. . . . 'They were without a vestige of the original uniforms. They had all been torn to pieces, and the men had made coats out of

---

The British Cavalry (Longmans, 1857)

their blankets, and trousers out of anything they could get. A tight, well-fitting jacket is all very well for a dragoon to wear whilst walking about a country town, or making love to nursery-maids, but this is not the purpose for which a soldier is intended, and real service should be the main object in view, both as regards his clothes and equipment'. He was later to reform the working-dress of the 10th Hussars, and never forgot the lessons learnt on the plains of South Africa.

It was not only Valentine who thought the uniforms quite unsuitable. It was reported that during the action against the Basutos some of the 12th Lancers' horses fell and refused to stand to be remounted. The enemy were close behind, and, except where comrades came back to hold the horses, many men were cut down as their overalls were too tight to enable them to mount alone.

The misery of the soldiers in this campaign was also described by another writer at the time (WR King, *Campaigning in Kaffirland*, (London 1853)) who said that the troops carried only three days' rations and one blanket. When the rainy season arrived, he wrote:

> It was in vain the shivering horses turned their tails to the storm or the drenched and shapeless heaps of humanity stretched on the ground, pulled their wet blankets more closely round them, for the pelting storm and searing wind were not to be avoided, and a day of excessive fatigue to the men was succeeded by a night of sleepless discomfort.

With some sarcasm, a correspondent wrote: 'The use of the lance over all other weapons was now evident, for the men, striking two of them into the ground and with another passed horizontally through the loops and a blanket stretched over it, found most excellent and convenient tents'.

They often had to march through thick forest, studded with huge rocks, and through thorny dense undergrowth – well-known to the Kaffirs, but quite foreign to the British Cavalry. Even so, the 12th Lancers were not down-hearted. 'Minié' rifles were distributed to the officers as a great improvement on the old 'Brown Bess' – although the men were still armed only with the lance and a pistol.

This first experience of life in the field made an indelible impression on Valentine. However splendid the accoutrements of the Regiment and however perfect the drill on the parade-ground, he would never forget that the true objective of the Army was to be ready at all times for active service, and that cavalry must always be ready for swift action should the occasion arise.

Meanwhile, the fortunes of war in South Africa had changed. The Governor determined to clear the Watercloof, and divided his attending force into three columns under Colonels Michel, Eyre and Napier. The 12th Lancers were stationed at Elenor Post to intercept any enemy withdrawal, and on 10 March the troops advanced. Many cattle and some prisoners were captured by the Twelfth and the Kaffirs were pursued to the River Kei. The victory, however, came too late for Harry Smith. In the summer he was replaced by General Cathcart (who was later to lose his life in the Crimean War). The new Governor decided to rest both men and horses who were by now exhausted.

In the Autumn Cathcart turned his attention to the Basutos, perhaps the fiercest of the tribes, who had driven their cattle to the summit of the Beria plateau. At first, the General camped at Platberg, and was visited by the great chief Mosesh himself, escorted by his warriors. The Basuto horsemen were described by Major Tylden at the time:

> The Basuto horseman carried his musket slung over his right shoulder, and a leather bucket carrying assegais, knobkerrie (a club) and a special barbed spear for disembowelling his wounded enemy, over his left shoulder. In his right hand he carried a light axe with a half-moon blade, mounted on a two foot handle, weighing up to three pounds and very sharp. It was used like a sword, but could be thrown at close range with deadly effect.

They were formidable enemies, and after a conference with their chief, Cathcart decided that they could not come to terms and decided to sweep the Beria plateau. Colonels Eyre and Napier were to close in while a force under Colonel Tottenham, which included young Lieutenant Valentine Baker, was to act as rearguard.

Colonel Tottenham was watering his horses at 'Soldiers' Spring' when the Basutos suddenly closed in upon him and his men. The lance was no good at close quarters and they had to cut their way out with their swords, as they were by now surrounded. Colonel Tottenham behaved with great distinction – 'The last man to return' wrote one of his party, 'he remained almost the last in the retreat, and by cool courage and good riding, managed to save the life of a sergeant major by shooting a Basuto who was just about to stab him'.

Tottenham checked his retreat at a stone wall. He was now on foot with a wounded man on his horse. However, at last, with some re-inforcements from Napier, he was able to drive off the enemy. Such unselfish courage was typical of the man and won the devotion and admiration of his young lieutenant. Although hit on the head by a knobkerrie, the official report ran, 'It did not mitigate his ardour or destroy his coolness in action.' That very night Mosesh submitted.

After crossing the Orange river soon afterwards, the 12th Lancers were ordered to leave South Africa and to set sail for India. They had acquitted themselves well. Valentine was described as having 'distinguished himself with gallantry' at the siege of Beria and was awarded a medal with two clasps. Punch, Valentine's gallant little Cape horse, sailed with his master to Madras. 'My only fear,' wrote Valentine, 'used to be lest he should get ill from over-feeding, for Punch was a great favourite on board ship, and managed to get a larger allowance of food than pleased me.'

★　★　★

The Twelfth were to be stationed at Bangalore, in the native state of Mysore. It was one of the most romantic and attractive parts of Southern India. The long lines of tents and white bungalows in which the men were to live, were surrounded by brilliant flowers – hibiscus, purple bougainvillaea, and brilliant red canna lilies, while tropical palm trees, frangipani and wild rhododendron trees showed that the forests of Mysore were not too far away. These were forests where tiger and samba could be hunted, and where herds of elephants could be seen at night coming down to drink at the forest pools.

An added attraction was the Stud owned by Major-General Cubbon, in which horses were bred for the Army, and which was then situated on the outskirts of Bangalore.

The cool early morning sunshine gave a perfect setting for cavalry drill and horse management, leaving the long afternoons free for the 'siesta' so much needed by horses and men alike. It was during these periods of enforced rest that Valentine had time to study his favourite subject, the breeding and management of horses. Just as Winston Churchill, stationed at Bangalore some forty years later, was to find time to read Gibbon's *Decline and Fall*, Valentine Baker was able to study in particular the colonial horses he found in India. He wrote later:

> Our Indian Empire is directly dependent on importation for its supply . . . the numerous Cavalry [regiments] are mainly supplied by annual importation from the Persian Gulf, the Cape, Australia and Government breeding studs.
>
> The horses, brought down from the Gulf are of four descriptions, viz. Arab, Gulf Arabs, Persians and Herats. These are the most prized horses in India.

17

He described how the Gulf Arabs were a cross between the Persian and Arabian, but 'with a loss of that appearance of extreme high breeding which denotes the pure Arab'. He thought nothing of the Herats, however: 'A very coarse description of the Persian, but much less compact, and generally very fretful, vicious and delicate.'

He found the stud-bred horses in India varied, increase in size leading to a falling off in stamina and 'bone'. He was later to recommend that a 're-mount establishment' should be formed in the Persian Gulf, so that better horses might be obtained than those brought down to India by the Arab dealers. He was much helped in his studies and advised by General Cubbon who not only owned the stud at Bangalore but was also the Commissioner for the State of Mysore.

A tribute to the 12th Lancers, while stationed at Bangalore, was paid by Captain Henderson, who had transferred from the 15th Hussars. He wrote:

> My experience of the men of the 12th are of the hardiest, healthiest and finest set of fellows for service it has ever been my good fortune to behold . . . Their smartness and soldier-like bearing could not be excelled, or their riding. The latter I have never seen equalled, their long service at the Cape had brought them, as we say of a race-horse, 'as fine as a star and as fit as a fiddle' for roughing it in any part of the world.

For recreation, there were race-meetings, always popular with the Cavalry, cricket matches and hunting the jackal, also shooting and exciting hunting expeditions into the jungle. Polo had not yet been introduced – in fact, it was not until 1870 that a description of the game, as played by the Maripur tribe, reached England through an article in *The Field*. The first game ever played in England was by members of the 10th Hussars at Aldershot, where golf clubs and billiard balls were used.

4

THE CRIMEA

Whilst the 10th Hussars and 12th Lancers were stationed in India, the storm clouds were gathering over Europe. The great Duke of Wellington had died in 1852, his death marking the end of an era. The Army, perfected in discipline and drill, was perhaps the most envied in Europe, its uniforms the most dazzling, its officers the most respected – but over thirty years of comparative peace at home had brought few real changes. The Purchase system, so bitterly decried later, was still in force in England, and had been considered by Wellington himself as perfectly acceptable. He took the view that the system 'brought into the Service men who have some connection with the interests and fortunes of the country besides the Commission which they hold from Her Majesty' and so prevented the British Army from being mercenary in character. Although purchase would be abolished in 1870, the reform was slow in coming and there was a good deal of bitter opposition within the country, not only towards those who were responsible for its retention but even towards officers who had acquired promotion under the system. Valentine Baker would experience that opposition at the time of the personal crisis that would change his whole life, some years later.

Other reforms were equally slow to be introduced and the life of the private soldier was extremely hard. In many respects the Army still clung to the old traditions which had been so successful at Waterloo. It was only in such books as *Cavalry – its History and Tactics* and *Nolan's System for Training Cavalry Horses* by Captain Lewis Nolan that the old traditions were criticised.

Captain Nolan was one of the most brilliant young cavalry officers of his time. His father had been British Vice-Consul in Milan, and he had been brought up in the military academy there, becoming an outstanding horseman even at the early age of fourteen. He was noticed by an officer of the Austrian Imperial Guard, and given a commission in a crack Austrian Cavalry Regiment. Later, from loyalty to his own country, he joined the 15th Hussars, and visited Russia, France and Germany studying their methods. In 1854 he was ADC to General Airey, who was Quarter Master General to the Commander-in-Chief, Lord Raglan.

Nolan's views on horse management, and on the foolishness of too much brilliance in dress were those with which Valentine Baker would have entirely agreed. 'Of what use' wrote Nolan, 'are plumes and bandoliers, sheepskins and sabretaches in war? Never believe that our Hussar uniform is the proper dress in which to do Hussar's duty in war, to scramble through thickets, to clear woods, to open the way through forests, to ford or swim rivers, to bivouac – to be ready always on outpost work, to 'rough it' in every possible manner'. After the war, when he was writing his own plain-spoken and important book (see page 35), Valentine would be greatly influenced by Nolan's work.

But the revolutionary views of Captain Nolan, on dress and horse-management, were little heeded in 1854, and the cavalry regiments which embarked for the Crimea were woefully short of serviceable clothing, tents and every sort of equipment needed for the wild and barren country on which they were to land.

Even the upright 'Cavalry Seat' which had been introduced first from the Continent for men carrying the lance, was still in fashion in the early 1850s, and the weapons were still the same, with the re-introduction of the lance, itself, beside the breech-loading carbine.

During the last few years, it was true, some slight effort had been made to reduce the hardship of service for the soldiers themselves. Flogging had been reduced to a maximum of 50 lashes in 1847; schools for children of the soldiers had been started, drink was no longer sold in the mess, and for the horses, a veterinary surgeon had joined the black-smiths and farriers who normally followed the cavalry. But there was still overcrowding in the men's quarters, and the pay of the soldiers barely covered their expenses.

It was not only in their conditions and their equipment that the Army was not progressive. The Generals, and many of the officers, were of the 'Old School'. General Raglan himself, the Commander-in-Chief, had served under the Duke of Wellington for forty years. He was now sixty-seven years old. Both Lord Lucan and Lord Cardigan, those handsome brothers-in-law, who could never agree, held old-fashioned and out of date views at the start of the campaign – and these were also held by senior cavalry officers in the Crimea.

Such was the force that sailed in 1854 and was to arrive in Varna in the Spring. Magnificent to look at, splendid in courage and drill, but lacking in the equipment needed for a long campaign in the Middle East, and very open to illness, dysentery and cholera.

The Allied Army landed at Kalamita Bay on 14 September, 1854. Fighting beside the French at the Alma, the British forced the Russians back upon Sebastopol; then, making a flank march, the Allies took up a position on the south side of the fortress, the British occupying Balaclava.

It was thought later, by Sir Winston Churchill, that a swift attack from the north might have taken Sebastopol by storm, and thus rendered the whole long siege unnecessary, but against the advice of Lord Raglan, the French Generals insisted on marching to the south.

On 25 October, following a Russian attack, the cavalry engagements which took place which are now part of our history. The successful attack by the Scarlett's Heavy Brigade on the Russian cavalry, and the terrible and disastrous charge of Cardigan's Light Brigade in which Captain Nolan lost his life, are now well-known. Captain Nolan, whom Valentine Baker so much admired, was at that time General Airey's Aide de Camp, and it was he who was asked to deliver Lord Raglan's order to Lord Lucan, which ran: '*Lord Raglan wishes the Cavalry to advance rapidly to the front, follow the enemy and try to prevent the enemy carrying away the guns. Troop horse artillery may accompany. French Cavalry is on your left. Immediate. R. Airey.*'

In sending this rather enigmatic message Lord Raglan no doubt meant the British Naval guns, with which the redoubts had been armed, and which the Russians were re-taking. They were not visible from the valley. Captain Nolan rode at a gallop down the steep incline and delivered the message to Lord Lucan. As Lord Lucan hesitated a moment, for the only guns which he could see were those of the Russians, Nolan's hand swept out. 'There my Lord, is your enemy, there are your guns!'

Lord Lucan then himself took the message to Lord Cardigan who did not hesitate. Drawing his sword, and in the full dress uniform of the 11th Hussars, he rode slowly forward, a few yards ahead of his Brigade, after giving the order to advance. It was a superb example of courage. Only a few moments later, as the whole Brigade moved slowly forward at a trot, Nolan realised that a terrible mistake had been made, and he rode suddenly out in front of them with his arm raised, as if to give some message. But already the enemy guns were firing and a piece of shrapnel struck him through the heart. The message was never given, and the Light Brigade advanced, in perfect order, without flinching, towards the Russian guns. . . .

Nolan's loss to the British Cavalry was incalculable, for he was one of the foremost exponents of the cavalry arts, despite his youthful rank. Fortunately Valentine was to follow closely in Nolan's footsteps with his own writing in the years ahead. Nolan's recommendations and innovations based upon his studies and practical experience in the field were to be the foundation of much of Valentine's writing in the years ahead, and were to meet with great success and be very widely adopted.

* * *

One can imagine the agony of impatience which possessed the two regiments still in India, when the news filtered through. The 10th had been stationed at Kirkee for five years. The 12th Lancers, although only recently arrived in India, could hardly bear to hear of their comrades in the 8th and 17th who had so gallantly lost their lives in action.

As early as July, Colonel Parlby had suddenly galloped on to the cricket pitch at Kirkee, waving despatches announcing that the 10th Hussars had been ordered to the Crimea. The news had been greeted with loud cheers but the excitement was shortlived, for the orders were soon countermanded. Now, following on from the terrible description of the casualties sustained in October, new orders had, at last, come through and both the 10th Hussars and the 12th Lancers sailed for Suez early in 1855.

The 12th Lancers had left Mysore in two Divisions. The first was under Colonel Pole, and the second Colonel Tottenham, in whose division Valentine was proud to serve. They marched through Seringepatan and Mysore to the Malabar Coast and, while the troops were embarking the horses it was said that they found the sun so hot that they tied their shirts round their heads as turbans. The heat was intense in the fifteen days passage to Aden, and for the following six days until they disembarked at Suez. 'The horses', wrote Henderson, 'were most carefully tended, groomed and handrubbed. We had the veterinary surgeon on board, and under his management we had not a single sick horse all the passage. . . . Every morning we washed a certain number in salt water.'

The ships, laden with equipment, horses and baggage, at length arrived safely at Suez. Colonel Tottenham was now put in charge of the first division, and with Valentine, now a Captain, set out on the long march to Cairo across the desert. This had to be undertaken by night, and was to test the endurance and ingenuity of both the 10th Hussars and the 12th Lancers, who followed them.

Two officers had gone on ahead and several hundred camels had been commandeered to carry the supplies and stores. These must have added to the eeriness of the march across the shifting sand – the horses with their jangling bits and gleaming equipment flashing in the moonlight, with the dark shapes of the lurching camels following them. Alone, walking ahead, an Egyptian guide, in his long white djallaba, holding a single lantern on a very long pole, guided the cavalrymen across the mysterious desert, their only other guide being the stars.

In addition to the difficulty of travel in the cool hours of darkness was the difficulty of picketing the horses by day. 'Picketing pegs', as used in India, were of no use in the desert sand and many horses at first broke loose, until it was decided to sink empty sacks, weighted with sand, into the ground, attached to the ropes securing the horses: Valentine Baker was to write later in his book *The British Cavalry*:

> The French plan, as adopted by the Chasseurs d'Afrique, of fastening each horse by one foreleg to a stout rope and peg is handy, but the ground will not always hold the pegs, and then there are no means of fastening the horses except by linking, which deprives them of rest. The plan I would recommend would be to carry a strong rope for each troop . . . The end of this rope should be fastened to a bush, or stick, and buried about two feet deep. This is more secure than any pegs and less likely to draw.

Eventually, the two regiments arrived in Cairo. The 12th Lancers were to follow the 10th to Alexandria. After resting at Abbassia, a barracks just outside Cairo, they embarked in April for Constantinople and the Crimea. Valentine was put in charge of the embarkation of the horses. After describing the arrangements for the horses' comfort in detail, he wrote:

> The quickest embarkation that ever came under my observation was in the case of a detachment of 280 horses of the 12th Lancers, embarking at Alexandria, for the Crimea, in the steamer *Etna*. We commenced embarking at 7 am. The horses had to be sent out in boats at a distance of one mile, nevertheless by 1 pm every horse was in his place on board ship. I timed the slinging of some of these horses, and so expert were our men at their work, that some were slung, lowered and in their stalls in fifty-one seconds, whilst a whole boat-load was got on board, at an average of fifty-six seconds per horse.

He added, 'I have invariably remarked that well-bred horses are more easily embarked than those coarsely-bred. This is particularly the case with Arabs, and I have seen the most fiery and spirited animal led quietly into a boat without making the slightest opposition.'

*   *   *

The 10th Hussars, soon to be followed by the 12th Lancers, disembarked at Balaclava on 19 April, 1855. Both regiments were amazed at the welcome they received. Officers and men from the Front, gaunt and haggard after a depressingly cold winter with scanty resources of shelter, food and clothing, gathered on the quay, and showed their admiration of the beautiful Arab horses, and the soldierly bearing of the men.

As soon as the final orders had been given to embark for the Crimea, Colonel Parlby of the Tenth had given orders to abolish pipeclay and razors – so that the men, with their beards, buff belts, slings and gloves 'looked more like old campaigners than soldiers newly arrived in the field', as William Howard Russell, *The Times* correspondent in the Crimea described them.

Very soon the officers of the 10th Hussars and 12th Lancers discovered that the Cavalry Division which they were to join was so decimated that there were scarcely enough men to mount a squadron. Valentine wrote 'No-one, who was not present, can form any conception of the British cavalry in the Crimea, during the summer of 1855. Young, weakly, half-drilled recruits were sent out, who could barely sit on, much less manage, a horse properly. Half the force that turned out with the British Cavalry on the day of the Tchernaya, 16 August 1855, was composed of untried, undisciplined boys of this description.'

On 24 May, soon after their arrival, the whole of the British cavalry was reviewed on open high ground above the sea. The 10th Hussars and 12th Lancers contributed 800 sabres out of a total of only 1,400. The tragic Light Brigade, could only muster about 100 men in all, and Valentine wrote 'Balaclava annihilated the Light Brigade . . . notwithstanding all the exertions made in England, and a summer passed in perfect inactivity, not a single regiment except the 10th and 12th from India ever again reached an effective strength.' He was later to recommend fewer and larger regiments, with training depots attached to them, so that the strength of the regiments could be kept up when on Active Service.

Immediately after the parade, a reconnaissance, under the direction of the Turkish general Omar Pasha, was made to ascertain the strength of the Russians on the river Tchernaya. To Valentine it was heartrending to ride over the plain extending from Balaclava to the Tchernaya – broken remains of sabretaches, harness and uniforms bore witness to the battle of 25 October the year before. One cannot help feeling that when Valentine was writing his important book, *The British Cavalry*, two years later, it may perhaps have been this terrible scene that inspired him to recommend a much simpler and more sensible form of dress for the cavalryman and lighter accoutrement for the horses.

The Times' correspondent, WH Russell vividly described the scene:

> As the force moved on, evidence of the fatal and glorious 25 October became thick and painful. With the crash of drums and the shrill strains of the fife, with the champing of bits and the ringing of steel, man and horse swept over the remnants of their fellows in all the pride of life. The Scots Greys and Inniskillings, the 4th and 5th Dragoon Guards, all had been there, and the survivors might well feel proud, when they thought of that day. The 10th Hussars were conspicuous for the soldierly and efficient look of their men and the condition of their light, sinewy and showy horses.

It had been due to Russell's reports that those at home had first become aware of the disasters in the previous year, the privations suffered by the soldiers before Sebastopol during the long, freezing winter and the terrible disaster when the Bosphorus flooded and the tents had been blown to shreds, and when every vessel in the harbour had been destroyed including the *Prince*, bringing comforts to the shattered army. These reports had inspired a question by a private member in the House in February 1855, and had actually led to the downfall of the Government, the succession of Palmerston as Prime Minister, and the establishment of the now famous 'Sanitary Commission' sent out to report on the conditions in the Crimea. 'We were saved by the Sanitary Commission' were words attributed to Florence Nightingale at this time. By the time the 10th and 12th arrived she had already transformed the hospital at Scutari. The terrifying, enormous building, which in the Autumn had reeked with infection from cholera, and where soldiers had died more from this infection than their wounds, was now purified and disinfected – by her efforts and those of her nurses alone. The death rate which had been forty per cent had been reduced to twenty-two per thousand. Though ill herself, Miss Nightingale worked valiantly on. In the summer of 1855 she was taken to the heights above Sebastopol from where she could look down on the beleaguered city.

It was said that Lord Raglan, so near to death himself, wanted above all things to see her. He was afraid that if he sent in his name, she would refuse to receive him – but he knew that she would do anything for a simple soldier. He went to her tent and when asked who he was, he said 'A soldier'. Florence, too ill to rise, welcomed him and they talked together for quite a while, to his great satisfaction.

Meanwhile the cavalry regiments were employed on reconnaissance, outpost and orderly duties. Young Captain Baker soon realised the strain put upon the dragoons, who were suddenly ordered to leave the flanks of squadrons as skirmishers, and who were too heavily laden or exhausted to undertake outpost duty, especially at night. He was later to recommend a special troop or squadron of light cavalry for this most important task – similar to the light troops used on the Continent.

On 25 May, the 10th Hussars and 12th Lancers, grouped under Colonel Parlby, acted as covering troops for the Allied Forces occupying the line of the Tchernaya, and then divided again. Valentine wrote that he served with the 12th Lancers for a time under the celebrated French General, General d'Allonville. It was his first experience of joint Allied operations, and he wrote:

> I remember being rather astonished at the orders of a celebrated French General; but though I fancied at the time that they savoured of foolhardiness, I afterwards saw the correctness of the general principle which dictated them. We had advanced from Eupatonia with a force of 4,000 French, English and Turkish Cavalry, and about 12,000 French and Turkish Infantry and 32 guns; the whole under General d'Allonville, and found the Russian outposts occupying the village of Sak. We came upon the Russian Army in very considerable force, and in a strong position. The whole country was one vast undulating plain or steppe, occasionally broken by ravines, and one of the largest of those separated the two armies. The horse artillery were brought to the Front, and for about half an hour a very pretty little artillery fight went on; but it was soon evident that the enemy were very superior, both in guns and weight of metal; whilst, from clouds of dust in the distance, it was very plain that a much larger force was in support, and that the six or seven thousand cavalry on our front were merely a portion of the Russian Army opposed to us. Night was also coming on, and we accordingly retired to the village of Sak, and encamped for the night, the enemy not attempting to cross the ravine, or follow us . . . To our surprise, General d'Allonville ordered the cavalry to unsaddle their horses, the men to pitch their tents, and everything to go on as if no enemy had been within ten miles – but he bestowed great attention to the outposts; and squadrons were ordered to patrol all night, in the direction of the enemy. All passed off quietly. No night attack was made, and horses and men were all the better the next day for this arrangement.

'Of course' wrote Valentine:

> . . . all our force were under arms long before daybreak . . . At the conclusion of the War we learnt from Russian Officers that on that very night an attack on our camp was debated. General Wrangel wished to charge right into the camp at the head of thirty Squadrons of cavalry, but Gortschakoff argued as our own General, and no attack was made . . . It is in these small points that a good General saves his men and horses, and has them in good order when really wanted. . . . At that time' he continued, 'we trusted mainly to the Turks and Bashi-Bazouks for the performance of outpost duties. English cavalry, as at present constituted, are utterly unfitted to bear the wear and tear of this kind of work. Imagine a horse carrying upwards of twenty stone, after a hard day's work, having to be out all night on outpost duty, and this repeated day after day. Very light men should perform these duties, for our present light cavalry would be ineffective in a week.

It was while the 12th Lancers were serving under the French General in June, and a few days after a minor assault on Sebastopol had failed, that the Army heard of the sudden death of Lord Raglan, the Commander-in-Chief. He was said to have died of 'Crimean fever' but many thought that he had died of a broken heart, disillusioned with a war which he felt could not conform to the exacting standards and discipline of the old 'Iron Duke' whom he had been so proud to serve, and saddened by the terrible losses of the cavalry in October the previous year. One of his last despatches was sent to the 10th Hussars sympathising over the death of one of their most beloved officers, Captain Bowles, who had died from cholera only a few weeks before. The 10th Hussars and the 12th Lancers were among those who provided the escort for Lord Raglan's body to be taken to HMS *Caradoc* at Kazatch Bay on 3 July.

★ ★ ★

There were now very few of the original gallant officers left in command of the cavalry. Lord Cardigan had sailed back to a hero's welcome in January and Lord Lucan himself was recalled on 14 February.

As Valentine soon discovered after his arrival in the Crimea, the cavalry regiments had been sadly mishandled throughout the campaign. At the Battle of the Alma, Nolan had begged Lord Lucan to commit the cavalry, but his pleas had been ignored. Later the view would be expressed that had the cavalry followed up the beaten enemy after that battle, the siege of Sebastopol might have been avoided. As Valentine himself witnessed, a golden opportunity for the cavalry was lost at the Battle of Tchernaya when the heavy dragoons were held back, denying them the chance of taking a leading part in the victory.

Valentine himself had been noticed during the campaign. His initiative and gallantry had been appreciated, and on the recommendation of Colonel William Heathcote Tottenham of the 12th Lancers, he was recommended for service with the Commander-in-Chief's escort.

At length, on 8 September, after a tremendous bombardment from the Allied guns, Sebastopol was once more attacked and as night fell the walls, earthworks and redoubts, so firmly established by the famous Russian engineer, Todleben, at last gave way, and were breached. The triumphant but exhausted Allied Army poured into the city. The smoking ruins and buildings were practically deserted as the 12th Lancers and 8th Hussars, among the first to enter the city that night, galloped through the dark and treacherous streets and Valentine was proud to be with them. Most of the inhabitants had streamed from the city to the north, following the Russian garrison in their retreat, but many of the buildings were mined, and just as dawn broke two large forts crumbled into ruins. The ships in the harbour had all been sunk and when the southern side of Sebastopol fell, it was little more than an empty shell.

By an amazing chance, Valentine's younger brother, James, also rode in among the first – with the 8th Hussars. It seemed a miracle that he had not taken part in the fatal charge of the Light Brigade the year before. The 8th had suffered terrible casualties that day, but, earlier, a small detachment had been detailed to form an escort to Lord Raglan on the Heights overlooking the valley, and James had been among them. Now the brothers met at last, both mounted and flushed with the moment of victory. They swore to meet again as soon as possible, and strangely enough, this was very soon to occur.

* * *

During the following winter both the 12th Lancers and the 8th Hussars were sent to Scutari on the Bosphorus, which was also the Headquarters of the Hussar Brigade for the winter. Parlby, now a Brigadier General and in command of the Brigade, was to return to Scutari early in the spring.

The winter was to pass off peacefully, but a squadron of the 10th, together with the Chasseurs d'Afrique, both under the command of

Osman Digna, were sent to support Sir George Brown at Kerch. Although this action resulted in an orderly retreat, General Simpson was to write afterwards – 'Nothing could exceed the coolness and courage of the troops in the presence of such overwhelming numbers of the enemy.' The cavalry regiments continued to perform the duties of outpost in the neighbourhood of Kerch until peace was proclaimed.

At Scutari, the days were spent in military exercises and the supervision of the welfare of men and horses. Valentine and James decided to share a small Turkish house, on the banks of the Bosphorus, and Colonel Tottenham, to their great delight, offered to join them. Not far away, there were still members of the 12th Lancers and 10th Hussars in the great hospital at Scutari, ill from cholera that winter, as well as the wounded, and they were among the many soldiers who, but for the devoted nursing of Florence Nightingale and her staff, would have died. Indeed, during her convalescence in the Chaplain's house at Scutari, Miss Nightingale was still tireless in organising the sanitation and equipment of the hospital – often visiting the wards herself. She organised a reading room for the men who were able to walk, and in January 1856, she was writing to a Chaplain to say 'she had just seen Thomas Whybron, 12th Lancers, and that he had promised me that he will not only write to his wife, but transmit money to her through me, after the first of next month. She had better write to him herself, and send her letters through me.' No detail seemed too small for her attention.

Meanwhile, in the evenings, with Colonel Tottenham to guide him, Valentine studied the works of Captain Nolan and Youatt, an equally well-known expert on cavalry drill and horsemanship. He was to find in their writings many of the answers to the questions which had been pressing so deeply on his mind ever since his experience in South Africa. The disasters as well as the triumphs of the Crimean War had made a deep impression upon him – the terrible price paid for the long, drawn-out siege of Sebastopol, the effects of inadequate food and clothing upon the soldiers throughout the bitter winter, resulting in the devastating epidemic of cholera and other sickness which carried off so many officers and men. All this gave him much to ponder over as he began to correlate the notes that he had so carefully prepared after his service in India, Africa and Turkey. These he now compared with the conclusions drawn in Nolan's works.

The winter provided a delightful interlude in which to rest in the Turkish house with his brother and his Colonel. The weather was fine after the terrible storms of the previous winter, and the Bosphorus lay before them, shining and sparkling in the sunshine, crowded with ships, bringing in supplies and reinforcements.

Everyone hoped that the War would soon be over, and the brothers were delighted, especially when they had a letter to say that their elder brother, Sam, was about to arrive for a visit.

They were, however, shocked to hear his news. His patient young wife, Henrietta, had become ill in Ceylon, and on their return to Europe, she had died after only a few weeks. Sam had been inconsolable, and had not known how to take the shattering blow. At last, hearing that his brothers were in Scutari, he determined to take ship and join them – and this he did.

In a letter, heavily disinfected, he wrote on arrival to his sister:

> Our troops are in fine health and condition. The French, on the contrary, are in a bad state, 4,500 in hospital! If the War should last, and not an hour passes without some fine steamer coming in full of troops, which looks very like War, although everyone says we are certain of peace – old England will come out strong after all. But I believe peace is certain.

It was at Scutari that Valentine and Sam together perfected a pistol and ball suitable for use by cavalry, even when riding at a gallop. The ball, invented by Sam, had the advantage of never shaking loose from the barrel, and the pistol Valentine had tried for several years. It was a long-barrelled weapon on the Whitworth principle, which, Valentine wrote, 'never gets out of order and answers perfectly'.

During the long winter evenings, the three brothers, so fortuitously thrown together, as much by chance as by design, would fling aside their cloaks, and in the light of oil lamps and guttering candles, would sit round the rough wooden table by the Turkish stove, discussing their plans for the future, in the light of all that had happened since the outbreak of war. All three agreed on the threat which still hung like a dark cloud over Europe, and all three were determined to travel to Turkey, Persia and beyond to discover how real was the danger from Russia which could not only threaten Britain's routes to the East but to India in particular, should Russia attempt an invasion of Afghanistan.

When peace came, with the Treaty of Paris, signed at the end of March 1856, whilst the immediate causes of conflict were removed, it provided no permanent settlement of 'The Eastern Question'. Russia surrendered Southern Bessarabia and her claims to a protectorate over the Turkish Christians: the Dardanelles were closed to foreign warships, as they had been before the War, and Turkey's independence was guaranteed by the Powers. But the fundamental weakness of Turkey was unaltered, remaining a temptation to Russian Imperialists intent on expansion.

Sadly, the brothers, who had so firmly cemented their friendship, had to part. Sam, after his return to England, was the first to fulfil their ambition and to travel in Turkey. In the next few years he was to help in the construction of the first railway across the Dobrushka to the Black Sea. James was to go up to Cambridge and Valentine to return home with his regiment.

★   ★   ★

Perhaps the most painful thing, for both the officers and their men, was the parting from their beautiful little Arab horses, which had carried them so well, and had proved themselves 'such good campaigners'. They were ordered to be made over to the Turkish Government on 20 May – a very sad day for the 10th Hussars and 12th Lancers. To say 'Farewell' to horses which they had bought and trained in India, ridden over the shifting desert sand from Suez to Port Said, and which had carried them so gallantly all through the Crimean Campaign was a bitter blow.

In the cavalry, every man usually had his own especial charger; Colonel Liddell was to write of the horses in India –

> It is possible to keep the same man permanently in charge of the same animal – it became a rule that a man was never to be parted from his horse, unless it was absolutely necessary on some good ground, either for service purposes or an accusation of bad conduct and neglect of his horse, on the part of the man. The consequence was that in the course of time each man came to look upon his particular troop horse as his own property, and called him by a pet name, in addition to the name given by the troop officer.

Miraculously, perhaps because he was a 'Cape' horse, rather than an Arab, the sturdy 'Punch' escaped, and was brought home to England, to enjoy many more happy years in his master's service.

★   ★   ★

There was a tremendous welcome for the army on its return to England, and in the official history we read that 'the 10th were greeted with enthusiastic and hearty cheers'.

On 8 July, the Queen herself inspected a march past, of 'the largest force of Britishers assembled in England since the battle of Worcester'. In her Diary, she described the uniform she wore to welcome her returning army:

> . . . a scarlet military tunic with gold braid. Brass buttons and a gold and crimson sash, a navy blue skirt piped with white, and a round felt hat with a white and scarlet plume, crimson and gold hatband, and gold tassels.

She was mounted on her favourite horse, Alma, and gave a moving address to the troops. Afterwards, they filed past her, and many were even permitted to touch her hand. The Queen was immensely moved by this personal contact with the returning heroes of the Crimea.

It was during these festivities and celebrations that Valentine realised that he had come to a turning point in his career. He could either return to India with the 12th Lancers, or transfer to his original regiment, the 10th Hussars. Perhaps it was due to the advice and recommendation of his Commanding Officer, Colonel Tottenham, whom he so much admired, that the transfer took place, and to the fact that Colonel Parlby, who had resumed command of the Tenth after commanding the Hussar Brigade in the Crimea, would have often met the young Captain at the winter Headquarters of the Brigade, at Scutari.

Valentine was now just twenty-eight years old. As we know, he had already fought in the Kaffir War, and had been awarded medals and clasps for his part in the battle of the Beria; he had taken part in the battle of the Tchernaya and the siege of Sebastopol. He had been singled out to serve in the Commander-in-Chief's escort, and was clearly an officer who would have a bright future in the cavalry before him.

But Valentine had begun to take a wider view. In the Crimea he had had an opportunity to see the French, Turkish and Russian cavalry in action. He had been able to compare their merits with those of his own country. He had witnessed the profound admiration of the Allies for the superb discipline and courage of the British under fire, and the desolation and despair following a battle.

He became quietly determined to share his conclusions with those in authority. His years of observation as a young subaltern and Captain could not be thrown away. He therefore decided to rejoin the Tenth and to apply for leave to study the military forces on the Continent, and especially their cavalry – determined to take the best from all that had been demonstrated on the field of battle, all that had been written, and to recommend it to the cavalry of his own country.

Meanwhile the 10th were reorganising at home. Colonel Parlby retired on 10 August, and was succeeded by Colonel Wilkie – the strength of the Regiment was being reduced (although soon to be increased once more on news of the Indian Mutiny), horses were being transferred from the Carabiniers and Light Dragoons. There was much training of new recruits and horses, and Valentine, before re-joining the Regiment, was given leave to visit the Austrian Army in their headquarters at Milan, and other European capitals. It was a magnificent opportunity to study Continental tactics and horsemanship at first hand.

Valentine was to study the system of 'non-pivot' drill, then used in the Austrian army, and to compare the different systems of cavalry training in France, Russia and Germany. Both his mentor Nolan's books (see page 19) had already become textbooks for the cavalry, and would later be adopted by the American Army as well. Perhaps it was Nolan's enlightened method of training horses by kindness which most appealed to Valentine. Nolan wrote that young horses should never be punished, or startled, but 'Teach them that acquiescence will be followed by caresses. There must be sympathy between man and beast'. It was exactly the method which appealed most to the young officer who was so soon to be promoted in the 10th Hussars.

5

A BOLD CRITICISM

On his return from Europe, in the autumn of 1856, and before taking up his engagement with his regiment, Valentine decided to write his book.

His father, Samuel, must have been delighted and proud to renew the acquaintance of his grown-up son, whom he had sent out to Ceylon so many years ago. The family had moved from Lypiatt Park, as his father had remarried, and with his second wife was now living in a comfortable house at Thorngrove, in Worcestershire, still within reach of all their former friends.

It is difficult to gather the reaction of the family to their new step-mother, but one story still survives. When young Sam returned from one of his travels, he found the great iron gates at the end of the drive at Lypiatt Park, had been closed against him and locked. Furious, he used his enormous strength to pull them from the gateposts and fling them to the ground, before galloping up the drive. The second Mrs. Samuel Baker must have found her step-sons rather difficult to under-stand. But no doubt the charming young cavalry officer would have enjoyed a warm welcome at his father's house, and we can imagine him sitting in the study, looking out over the quiet park and the chestnut trees, in the winter of 1856, with his books and notes round him, writing the slim volume based on his experiences in two wars, and which offered such a contrast to the quiet English scene before him.

Perhaps it was because of his delight in returning to England that Valentine began his book with a brief history of the English thor-oughbred horse. First, he wrote 'The quality of the cavalry of every nation must ever mainly depend upon the quality of the horses the country produces' and went on to say how far superior the breed of horses in England were to those of their Continental Allies.

He traced the distinctive breed of the English thoroughbred back to the time of James I, when, to the undying credit of that much discredited King, Arab blood was first introduced into the heavier breed of English horses. The King's ill-fated son followed him, but the popular Charles II may be said to have laid the foundations of the English thoroughbred by the introduction of four Arab mares.

Perhaps the most diverting of his conclusions is shown in the following sentence:

> The main stock of the best blood of the present day lay in the three following Eastern horses:– Firstly, the Byerly Turk, of whose origin little is known, but that he was introduced into Ireland in 1769. Secondly the Darley Arabian, imported by a Mr. Darley of Yorkshire, very early in the 18th century. Thirdly, the Godolphin Arab, which seems more properly to have been a Barb, and was first used as a sire in 1731.

There is almost the lilt of a poem or the introduction of a tale from the Arabian Nights in this description of the forebears of so many of the most famous of the racehorses of the early 19th century, although Valentine adds that 'care, feeding, and attention to "crossing" have done much to aid the present increase [in size].' He added: 'I much doubt whether the horses of any age have equalled in all points some of the celebrated horses of the last ten years.'

In all his thoughts, however, his beloved cavalry was all-important. He was shocked by the new trend for race-horse owners to breed a lighter, faster strain. He deplored the fashionable short races, taking the place of those which required more stamina – pointing out that the racehorses were the sires of the cavalry troop horses, and that there were no 'Government Studs' in England, such as he had found on the Continent, to produce suitable horses with more strength than speed, for the cavalry.

While he wrote, he no doubt was watching from his windows the swishing tails and firm hindquarters of his father's hunters, as they cropped the grass in the park, and also the sturdy compact figure of his own beloved 'Punch', delighting to spend the year in the lush Worcestershire countryside after his service abroad in two wars.

Later in the book, Valentine was to describe the huntsmen. 'With every pack of hounds in England, men of sixteen stone are to be seen superbly mounted on horses fully capable of carrying them even through the exercise of a trying run'. He felt that these magnificent horses could be bred both for the Cavalry and the hunting field. He wrote:

There is a rather general opinion that thoroughbred horses are more delicate than horses of coarser blood, but this I believe to be a popular error. No doubt the system of running thoroughbred horses as two-year olds has introduced a weak and weedy type of thoroughbred requiring great care, and incapable of bearing any degree of hardship. But many horses of the purest blood still combine great substance, power and bone; such animals are superior in endurance of every kind to the coarse, half-bred horse.'

He again recommended 'Punch' his Cape horse, saying: 'I am convinced that this kind of thoroughbred, crossed with the Cape horses of great bone and substance, would produce a small compact animal, unrivalled for light cavalry.' He recommended that the horses should not complete their training until they were four years old, but he felt that Government training establishments and studs, which would draft the horses to suitable regiments, would be far preferable to the method then in use, which depended largely upon the judgment of the Colonel of each individual Regiment – should the Colonel prefer light, speedy horses, they would be chosen for his regiment regardless of the weight of the dragoons, or vice versa.

Thus, in the first three chapters of his book, Valentine Baker had cheerfully plunged into the most controversial subjects concerning the cavalry of his day, challenging the breeders of cavalry horses, the race horse owners, and even the Colonels who selected the type of horse they wanted in their Regiment. He did not rest here. In the next few chapters he was to describe the equipment, dress, arms, saddles, swordsmanship and even 'the manoeuvres' of the cavalry, recommending in every case improvements which he had himself either drawn from his own experiences, or seen in Austria and on the Continent, in his recent travels.

First, he showed that a much more stable 'hunting seat' was to be preferred to the seat of the French and German cavalry, which was achieved mainly by balance. He described the cavalry seat then fashionable, and wrote:

> If we English are as a body the finest horsemen in the world – which seems evident – and understand more about horses, saddlery etc. than any other nation in the world, why should we not act upon our superior knowledge, instead of imitating those who are confessedly inferior to ourselves?

He recommended, next, a classification of the British Cavalry, that the heavy dragoons should ride the horses of 'considerable size, height and power', the men of more moderate size should be mounted on horses from 15.1 to 16 hands in height, and the lightest and smallest men who would be used for outpost duty, mounted on small, serviceable animals.

But perhaps his most important recommendation in the equipment of the cavalry was for the provision of carts, to transport sacks of corn for the horses, blankets and tents for the men, and to relieve the Hussar of much of the heavy equipment which even in the Crimean War he had been forced to carry when mounted. It was true that Marlborough and Wellington had organised their own 'Wagon Trains' to transport necessities for the army when in the field, but these Wagon Trains were unofficial and usually manned by civilians. Baker's account shows how little official transport was provided for the cavalry in the Crimean War.

To illustrate the importance of transport, he added up the weights of every piece of equipment which it was usual for horses to carry, and it came to an astonishing 21 stone and 4 lbs. He wrote:

> Even light horses, supposed to be capable of doing outpost duty, making forward marches and going at a rate of high speed for long distances, even charging where necessary, were forced to carry this enormous weight which often included not less than four days' corn, needed for the horses on active service. The use of carts would not only relieve the horses of weight, but also provide for carrying sick or wounded men, when on the march. . . . Had the British Cavalry in the Crimea been thus provided, the horses and men would never have perished in the winter of 1854. Even in the summer of 1855 the cavalry were almost entirely dependent on themselves for bringing up their own forage, and this was effected by slinging the sacks over the men's saddles, the horses being led. In my own Regiment alone, sixty men and horses were constantly employed upon this duty, and this rendered them non-effective for other purposes; whilst the men were fatigued by marching, loading and leading their horses under a burning sun . . . six carts and twelve men would have carried the same quantity of forage and performed the duty in a shorter time.

Perhaps it was largely due to this chapter in the book, that carts were actually introduced officially in 1862, and were in constant use afterwards. The 'Royal Wagon Train' of Wellington's campaigns was to develop into the Royal Army Service Corps which was later to become the Royal Corps of Transport. It would seem amazing to us now that the horses and men in the Crimea had to march under such tremendous difficulties.

The recommendation of the carts seemed naturally to be paralleled by a recommendation for a lighter, more serviceable, form of dress. With memories of the Kaffir war, and his own experiences there, the young Captain now recommended a much more serviceable 'monkey jacket' for wear on active service, describing minutely the clothing then issued to the Hussar, and simplifying it accordingly, whilst still advising a 'full dress' which should remain extremely smart for best occasions.

In his chapter on arms, he naturally paid tribute to the lance, but said that the 'Queen of Weapons' should only be placed in the hands of 'strong, picked men, and perfect horsemen.' He criticised 'the present guard, which is very defective.' He wrote of the cavalry swords then in use 'the sword, now generally used by the cavalry, could be much improved.'

In fact, in every chapter, he criticised, recommended changes and described possible improvements. Every detail of the men's kit, from socks and clothes brushes, curry combs and cooking tins, to swords and pistols came under his critical scrutiny. Above all he described the saddles then in use, recommending a much lighter, more serviceable type, comparable to a hunting saddle, rather than the cumbersome saddle then issued. He considered that: 'The Dragoons' saddle could be much lightened, if not made to take to pieces, as at present . . . I never could understand why it should be so made. Our ordinary hunting saddles never get out of order, and are easily cleaned, and why a Dragoon's should be a complication of movable straps, like a chinese puzzle, had ever been beyond my comprehension.' The lighter saddles would prevent sore backs and much hardship to the horses, besides reducing the cumbersome equipment.

He wrote too:

> I believe that the English have a greater love of horses than any other nation in the world; and although our cavalry soldiers have been accused of a want of affection for the animals they ride, I have never found this to be the case, unless they are harassed by an over-strained attention to them; but this is the fault of the Commanding Officer, and in the field, where it is impossible and unnecessary to obtain an extreme elegance of cleanliness. It only disgusts the men, and produces an exactly contrary effect to that intended. . . . It is little known in England with what respect and awe our troopers are regarded by the cavalry of other countries. They, of course, laugh at the numbers composing our regiments, and at the numerical strength of our cavalry altogether, but they have the greatest admiration for its composition.

Finally, in his chapter on Swordsmanship, he began:– 'Every Dragoon should be an expert swordsman, yet, strange to say, swordsmanship has hitherto been entirely neglected in our army.' He criticised the 'theatrical' system of attack and defence as carried out in cavalry riding schools, and described it as 'simply ridiculous'. He quoted a story told in the Crimea to illustrate this, of a young Dragoon who was wounded at Balaclava, and who, describing his encounter with a Russian officer, said: 'When he came at me, I gave him right defend, but the fool gave cut seven and hit me on the head, and down I went!' Valentine recommended a system of swordsmanship which had first been introduced into the Royal Navy, remarking: 'It is, like most things originated by sailors, soundly practical.' He recommended firearms for all Dragoons saying 'Dragoons should be taught to use their firearms with tolerable correctness, although mounted firing must ever be ineffective, and where both hands are required in the use of the weapon, accuracy is impossible.' He mentioned the Hottentots, who had taught their horses to stand still the moment their reins were dropped; but even then, he thought accurate firing from horseback was extremely difficult.

In spite of all these controversial opinions, Valentine was still very anxious that he should not be thought presumptuous in recommending any alterations to the established rules for the Cavalry. He wrote 'I trust I shall not be deemed pretentious, and should any suggestion emanating from it prove of ultimate advantage to the Service, I shall indeed feel amply rewarded.'

It was in his last six chapters that Valentine was to approach a far more sensitive subject then even those of arms, dress or equipment. He was to suggest a completely new form of regimental drill to a regiment whose traditions went back to the seventeenth century. He could not know that his new system of 'Non-Pivot Drill' adapted from the Austrian Army, was to be adopted, in a few years' time, throughout the Service. It was many years since the battle of Waterloo, and yet, he wrote, the drill in the cavalry had remained almost the same – perfect in precision and discipline, but woefully lacking in rapidity of movement. Thus, we were universally admired for the excellence of our horsemanship and courage, but the French and Austrians were already swifter in reaction to attack.

The alterations in drill which Valentine Baker recommended might seem complicated, but in fact they were a simplification of the system then in use. He wrote: 'The true principle of manoeuvring is to form a body of men in line, or column, in any given position, in the shortest possible time.' In fact, he would abolish many of the more complicated movements altogether. He wanted to do away with the concept of 'right and left front' and also of 'front and rear ranks'. The two should be interchangeable, depending on the situation. Thereby the need for countermarching would be avoided and, he argued, the men in the rear rank would become as much in the habit of working as those in the front.

In a series of diagrams, he showed how his plan could be used in the manoeuvres of a squadron, then in a regiment, stating that out of forty-five movements, fourteen could be entirely dispensed with, and many others simplified.

He then suggested the same economy of movement for a brigade, and wrote: 'All the advantages thus gained by this system in the movements of a regiment must be eventually trebly valuable in brigade movements.' He quoted Captain Nolan as saying: 'The art of manoeuvring consists of attacking your enemy at his weakest point'. But, he argued, 'to do this the complicated movements must be simplified.'

Even so, Valentine did not agree with Captain Nolan on every point. He could not agree that the employment of only one rank in cavalry formations was preferable to two ranks. He felt that in action, in a charge, the men would feel a lack of support, and weakness, without the immediate back-up of the rear rank.

He recommended this change in spite of the views of so great a soldier as the Duke of Wellington, who had written 'If the front rank should fail, and it should be necessary to retire, the second, or rear rank, is too close to sustain the attack and restore order.' But Valentine suggested that there was not so much chance of failure when the two ranks were employed. He wrote: 'No matter what the pursuit may be, there is a spirit of confidence engendered in every man, by feeling himself well-backed'. He added a note from his own brother, James' experience in the Crimea: 'A Squadron of the 8th Hussars at the retreat at Balaclava, formed in threes, pierced and rode in succession through the Squadrons of a Russian Regiment formed in column, and which had cut them off.' He felt in a single rank a bad morale effect would be produced on the men composing it.

To write in these terms must have needed great moral courage and daring on the part of so young an officer. Few had dared to disagree with the great Duke himself – Colonel Parlby, Lord Lucan and Lord Cardigan were still very active, while his own beloved Colonel Tottenham, who would no doubt have supported him through thick and thin, and to whom he dedicated his book, had unhappily died the previous year, on returning from the Crimea. But such was the temper of the hour, when the conduct of the war was so open to question and, since the reports of William Russell had opened the eyes of those at home to the terrible sufferings of our troops in the Crimea, that the slim volume was greeted with enormous enthusiasm when it was quietly published by Longmans in 1857. Valentine returned to the 10th Hussars in May of that year.

6

RAPID PROMOTION

The Commanding Officer of the 10th Hussars, when Baker returned to them, was Lieutenant-Colonel John Wilkie, who had at that time served with the Regiment for over twenty years. He had commanded the Regiment from its landing in the Crimea in 1855, when Colonel Parlby had been promoted to Brigadier and General Scarlett had received command of the Division. More recently, he had been complimented by the Duke of Cambridge on his training of new recruits, especially on the increase in numbers made necessary by the outbreak of the India Mutiny, and he was delighted to receive so experienced a young officer as Valentine, to assist him in his task. Colonel Wilkie at once recognised that Valentine possessed unusual ability. Years later, it was written:

> Valentine Baker had all the tastes and qualifications which peculiarly fit a man to distinguish himself as a soldier, and to impress his influence on others. He was an enthusiastic sportsman, a bold and determined rider, and he shared the daring adventurous spirit of his brother, Sir Samuel, the well-known traveller and administrator.

Only two years after rejoining the Regiment, Valentine was promoted to Major. In that year, the summer of 1859, army manoeuvres were held for the first time in Woolmer Forest. The cavalry were represented by a wing of the 10th under Major Baker. The army camped at Woolmer and remained for some days, and it is on record that the Queen herself visited the camp from 5–6 pm on the following Sunday, and 'after driving round the camp and partaking of the soldiers' bread and tea, returned to Windsor'.

At this time, the full dress of the Regiment, as published in the Regulations for 1855, was altered. The Hussar jacket, with pelisse and gold and crimson sash was abolished, and a 'tunic with skirt' was introduced. Badges of Rank were also introduced, for the Lieutenant Colonel, a crown, for the Major, a star, and for the Captain, a crown and star. The collar was still to be laced round the top with 'gold lace and figured braid', and the sleeve was still ornamented with knots of gold chain lace, and figured braiding eight inches deep.

Meanwhile Valentine's book *The Cavalry* had been published, and was much discussed in military circles. It became clear that, although very young for such swift and important promotion, no-one could have been better fitted to command the Regiment, on Colonel Wilkie's retirement, than the young officer who had studied and mastered the Continental form of drill and horse-management, and suggested such stringent improvements in the cavalry. In consequence, when Wilkie retired, Valentine was promoted to Lieutenant Colonel and, in 1860, given command of the Regiment at the age of thirty-three.

A tribute to Colonel Wilkie and to Valentine is paid by the official record: 'He handed over to his successor Colonel Valentine Baker, a regiment thoroughly disciplined and carefully drilled, and well-fitted to undertake those rapid movements introduced by that brilliant leader.'

It was just before Wilkie retired that Valentine introduced the first steeplechase to the Regiment, presenting a bronze challenge cup to the winner. It was an enormous success and it is interesting to note that the Veterinary Surgeon, Mr. Thacker, was to win twice, and so claimed the cup as his own in 1863. Valentine then presented another cup, a silver gilt Danish flagon, which would become the property of any officer who won three times.

The year 1860 was to become a very real challenge to the new Colonel. The 10th were inspected by Lord George Paget, their brigade commander in Aldershot, on 17 May, just three weeks after Wilkie's resignation. They were also present on 22 June at the Review in Hyde Park of the new Volunteer Forces, before the Queen.

On 11 July, the new Colonel introduced an innovation. He arranged for two squadrons of 120 men and horses, to embark and travel by train from Islington to Holloway Railway Station with one troop saddled, and one unsaddled. From there they were transported by train to Willesden Station 'on the London and North Western Line'.

Baker was determined to test this new and much faster means of travel for horses. It would mean so much to the Cavalry if successful. Like others of his generation, Valentine was fascinated by the invention of the steam train and all the developments of the railways. The trial proved an unqualified success.

That winter the 10th Hussars were stationed at Norwich, and an amusing incident is told of the visit of Major General Lawrenson, the Inspector General of the Cavalry, who came down to inspect them. He saw the line of jumps, erected by Valentine, to train the young horses, and immediately asked to watch the Regiment ride over them. The young colonel took the Regiment over in sections and General Lawrenson was so impressed that he insisted on leading the way, with his staff, on Captain the Hon. C. Molyneux' horse, 'Duchess'.

Later, the Regiment was to march to York, and there Valentine was to introduce his new system of drill in earnest. He had written that, although the British system of manoeuvres was better than those on the Continent, it was still faulty. He again stressed that the old system of drill had remained the same from the time of Waterloo and emphasised that more rapidity of movement was needed. He compared the French, who trained their cavalry officers in feats of endurance, with our infantry who, while unequalled in precision, were slow. With his own regiment under command upon which to practise the theories which both he and Nolan and, in particular, De Brach, had propounded in their writing, Valentine restated his view that the true principle of manoeuvre lay in forming '..a body of men, in line or column, in any given position in the shortest possible time'. Explaining that the new drill that he was introducing would only need slight alteration to movements then in use, he insisted that whilst he would not interfere with the mode of forming a squadron, it should be incapable of inversion and that there should be no named front or rear rank. Thus the 'non-pivot drill' which he had studied so carefully in Austria was introduced into the Tenth Hussars. The smartness of the Regiment and the increased swiftness and harmony of its drill movements greatly impressed all those officers privileged to see it. Baker would emphasise that of the forty-four movements in regimental drill, it had been possible to dispense with no less than fourteen. Many others had been simplified, giving a greatly increased power and facility of formation.

While stationed at York, and perfecting the new form of drill, the Tenth became very popular with the people of the town. They hunted with the local packs and even once put out a considerable fire, ruining some of their best uniforms. These were replaced by an Insurance Society which was actually run by Quakers. At their request, the payments were kept secret, as they did not want it known that they were rewarding the fighting men of the country. The Yorkshire Hussars, under the Earl of Harewood, went to York for their annual training, and adopted many of the movements recommended by Baker, who had been appointed their inspecting officer.

During that autumn, Valentine had a letter from his brother Sam who wrote from Turkey with the fascinating news that he was about to embark upon an expedition into the heart of Africa in an attempt to discover the source of the River Nile. He asked Valentine to arrange for his guns to be sent out to Cairo. These included his famous elephant gun which had so impressed Valentine in Ceylon. Sam had nicknamed it 'The Baby'; it had such a violent recoil that a man 'backing up' the hunter would himself also be thrown to the ground. Sam also asked for another favourite 'the little Fletcher', a gun that he would later take on all his explorations. Valentine arranged their despatch but, sadly, was unable to see his brother for another three years because his duties as Commanding Officer were to occupy all his time and energy.

In the following year, 1861, the news of the death of the Prince Consort was announced in November and the Tenth, led by their Colonel, were present at the memorial service held in York Minster. His death came as a great shock to the whole country and the nation went into mourning.

The popularity of the Regiment with the people of York had now become so great that the Mayor and Corporation granted the officers permission to build a boathouse and raft in 'The Lord Mayor's Walk'.

Two years later, a much greater honour was bestowed upon the Regiment. On the resignation of Earl Beauchamp as Colonel-in-Chief and his assumption of command of the Second Life Guards in April 1863, he was succeeded by His Royal Highness The Prince of Wales.

7

A ROYAL COLONEL-IN-CHIEF

Since the death of his father and his marriage to the beautiful Princess Alexandra of Denmark, the Prince of Wales had longed for greater responsibility in public affairs. So he was delighted when the Queen gave her consent to his appointment as Colonel-in-Chief of the 10th Hussars enabling him to follow in the footsteps of his great uncle, King George III. He at once threw himself into his new duties and became immersed in the organisation of the Regiment.

Perhaps it was fortunate that its Commanding Officer, Valentine Baker, had an enthusiasm which matched and even surpassed his own. The Prince recognised his dedication, and it was said in the official history: 'It was largely due to his encouragement and support that Colonel Valentine Baker's career with the Regiment proved such a successful one.' This loyalty and friendship never swerved on the part of the Prince, even when the days became darkest for Valentine. From the time spent with him in the Regiment, he knew Valentine's character perhaps better than anyone else, and the Prince's friendship, once given, never wavered.

Soon after the Prince of Wales assumed his appointment as Colonel-in-Chief, the Regiment was moved to Ireland, and nothing pleased Valentine so much as organising the transfer. He himself marched from York with Regimental Headquarters. As each squadron arrived at Liverpool, it proceeded at once to the docks, where the saddlery was packed in the cornsacks, and the horses were led on board a small hired transport. The Regiment disembarked at Dublin on 17 April and proceeded to the Royal Barracks, where, immediately, they began taking part in the Curragh Drill Season.

It was an ideal setting for the perfection of the non-pivot system of drill, and the formation of the squadron in three divisions of twelve fronts each, was introduced into the 10th. Official sanction was given for Baker to carry out the drill, and Major General Lawrenson, the Inspector General of Cavalry, came over to Dublin to inspect the Regiment once again.

The main duty of the cavalry at that time was to aid the civil power in the elections. The 10th were 'on duty' at Tralee, Clonmell and Tipperary, and these operations were extremely successful.

For relaxation, in the 'golden valley of Tipperary', there was hunting and shooting, and the 'Rock' Harriers near Cashel, with Captain the Hon. C.C. Molyneux as huntsman, and Lord Valentia as Whip, became well-known, while musketry practice was carried on at the Pigeon House Fort. It was either at this time, or in an earlier assignment to Ireland, that the amusing story grew up that 'The Tenth Don't Dance'. Apparently they were so lionised by the local dignitaries that the young officers invented this slogan to protect themselves from too many invitations.

Apart from their commitments in support of local government, the Regiment's tour in Ireland provided Valentine with a golden opportunity to train his troops in their new drill; many distinguished visitors from overseas and from other regiments continued to visit the 10th to study the non-pivot system in practice. There were, inevitably, more formal visits, involving the Regiment in ceremonial, such as the visit by their Colonel-in-Chief in 1865 to open the Dublin International Exhibition. He was accompanied by the Duke of Cambridge, Commander-in-Chief of the Army, and escorts for both were provided by the Regiment: the visit concluding with a Review by His Royal Highness in Phoenix Park. In the autumn, Valentine was promoted Brevet Colonel.

★ ★ ★

From his arrival in Ireland, the young Colonel was very conscious of a general discontent and unhappiness among the population. In spite of the repeal of the Corn Laws, following the disastrous potato famine, and measures by Lord Russell and succeeding Governors to ameliorate the conditions of the people, there was much real poverty and consequent discontent. Many of the Irish had fled to America, but at the end of the American Civil War in 1865, quite a number returned, with arms, ammunition and money, hoping to join the Fenians, overthrow the government and, eventually, to set up a republic in Ireland.

Secret societies or 'circles' had been formed, master-minded by James Stephens who, though arrested in Ireland, had escaped to Paris.

One of their most dangerous activities was to spread disaffection in the British Army stationed in Ireland. A Fenian Agent, however, one Jock Devoy, who had the task of introducing 'circles' into the British Army wrote: 'I succeeded very well with all the Regiments of the Dublin Garrisons except the 10th Hussars. They were picked men, at least physically: morally and mentally they were also above the average, which was not high, of the Army'. But even among those recruited to the 10th there was one influenced by the Fenians, a young man, Boyle O'Reilly, who was intelligent, active and well-educated and would have been a very promising recruit. But he daringly sewed the Insignia of the Movement under his sabretache and was at length discovered. He would have been executed, but Valentine intervened, and had him transported to Australia. There he escaped, and fled to America, where he later became a distinguished and respected newspaper correspondent!

On 5 March 1867, the Fenians finally rose, but the whole rising was a fiasco. The Commander-in-Chief of the movement in Ireland, General Massey, was arrested at Limerick Junction as he stepped out of the train to assume command. Meanwhile a 'flying column' under Valentine, consisting of fifty mounted and fifty dismounted men, had ridden out through snowstorms and pouring rain to protect the troops from Fenian attacks. On their return, Lord Strathnairn, then Commanding in Ireland, thanked the officers and men of the 10th for the good feeling displayed. He particularly mentioned the Thurles Flying Column, especially commending Colonel Baker.

It was during the tour in Ireland that Valentine introduced the Regimental Call from the opening movement of the 'Song of the Huguenots', which is often played to this day when the Regiment is on parade. He also introduced the playing of two hymns by the band every evening before the first and second Post of watch-setting, followed by the National Anthem. Everything Valentine did was designed to encourage a spirit of comradeship and regimental unity. That he succeeded in this would be clearly demonstrated some years later by the deep affection in which he was clearly held by all ranks despite the unhappy events which would so mar his life.

Not long before the Regiment ended its five year tour in Ireland, the Westley-Richards carbine, with which they had been issued on arrival, was withdrawn and replaced by the more modern Snider rifled carbine which had been converted to breech loading, a marked step forward. In April 1868, as they were making their final arrangements for their return in May, the Prince of Wales made another visit to the 10th.

During that visit, he was invested in St Patrick's Cathedral, with the Order of St Patrick – an occasion for which the Regiment again provided the escort. On 22 April, a grand ball was held in the Prince's honour in the Exhibition Palace – an event at which the 10th certainly *did* dance!

The good impression created by both officers and men of the Regiment during their Irish tour and their popularity with the local people is reflected by an entry in the Regimental History to the effect that, having left the Service, Captain Slacke was appointed as a Stipendiary Magistrate in Ireland.

★   ★   ★

While Valentine was keeping the peace in Ireland, Samuel had covered himself with glory in Africa.

The mystery which had surrounded the source of the river Nile had tempted many explorers to plunge into 'the Dark Continent' and it had been a quest after the heart of the adventurous Sam. He had been accompanied by his beautiful second wife, Florence, then only twenty-two years old. Together they had faced all the hardships of an expedition into the heart of Uganda. Almost alone, with only a few loyal natives to support them, Florence and Sam, after terrible adventures and illness, had finally reached a great lake, which they named the 'Albert Nyanza' after the Prince Consort, and which Samuel felt was of equal importance as a source of the great river as Lake Victoria, so recently discovered by Speke and Grant.

On his safe return to England, Sam was knighted by the Queen in the autumn of 1866. He and his young wife soon became the darlings of London Society. It was inevitable that, whilst staying with the Duke of Sutherland, they were to meet the Prince of Wales and his beautiful young wife, Princess Alexandra.

The Prince, who, of course, already knew Valentine well through his Colonelcy of the Regiment, gave Sam and Florence his unreserved friendship. There was only one cloud upon the horizon. When Sam asked Lady Wharncliffe if she would 'present' Florence at Court, on her marriage, the request was refused by the Lord Chamberlain. It now became clear that Queen Victoria did not in some way approve of the marriage. From early letters written whilst they were staying at Dunrobin Castle, it seems that the Queen thought they had not been married until their return to London in 1865. The Prince of Wales had written a quick rejoinder to his mother:

Dunrobin Castle
Sutherland
September 27th 1868

My dear Mama,

Sir W. Knollys wrote to me that you had heard Sir Samuel and Lady Baker were here, and that you wished me to know that she had been on intimate terms with her husband before she married. I had also heard the reports, and spoke to the Duke about it, and he assures me that he and the Duchess had made enquiries into the matter and they had no doubt that there was no foundation for the story, and the Duchess is very particular about the ladies she asks and would certainly not have asked Lady Baker to meet Alix unless she felt certain that she was quite a fit person to know.

She is one of the quietest most ladylike persons one could see, and perfectly devoted and wrapt up in her husband, and I think it very hard on both that this story should be believed, which must be most distressing for him, and very dreadful for her – and his name will always be known to history as a great discoverer. . . .

I remain

Your dutiful and affectionate son,
Bertie.

But the Queen was not convinced and from that time forward she mistrusted her son's friendship with Sam, and this made her more willing to believe the terrible scandal which was to surround his brother Valentine a very few years later.

His mother's anxieties about his friendships were only too well known to the Prince, but he was determined to make his own friends, and to recognise courage and enterprise wherever it could be found. He knew Sam as a first class shot and big game hunter, who spoke Arabic like a native and he admired him immensely. When, in 1868, he and Princess Alexandra planned to visit Egypt and take part in an exploring and shooting expedition on the Nile, he chose Sam as his guide to the expedition and to make all the arrangements, in spite of the fact that the Queen had written to him that she was distressed that the 'unprincipled' Sir Samuel Baker and the Duke of Sutherland were to be of the party. The Prince firmly replied that Baker, who had discovered the source of the Nile and was a good sportsman, knew the country well and 'whatever his principles be he is not likely to contaminate us in any way'. Later he wrote to his mother 'We find Sir Samuel Baker very agreeable and with so much to tell me about the country which no-one knows better than he does, that I cannot say how glad I am to have him to accompany me here.'

On his return from Ireland, Valentine found himself swept up in the society of his day. He, like his brother, was asked everywhere, and the Prince of Wales honoured him by making him a founder-member of his own Club, the Marlborough Club – to which many of the Prince's especial friends belonged.

The summer was a succession of balls and water parties, of theatres and dances, many of the famous beauties of the day remembered the tall, dark Colonel of 'the 10th' – and the beautiful Ettie Cowper, later to become Lady Desborough, often recalled her dances with him.

It was also during that summer that Valentine first met a man who would become a lifelong friend, Colonel Burnaby. He, too, was a member of the exclusive Marlborough Club, and the Prince of Wales was also Colonel-in-Chief of his Regiment, 'The Blues'.

Immensely tall and powerful, Burnaby possessed a magnetic charm. He appeared at times negligent and dilettante, but was in reality a superb horseman and immensely powerful fighter, both physically and morally. Only a few years later he was to make his historic ride to Khiva through the Russian lines – but in 1868 he was in London, publishing, with his friend Tommy Bowles, the first edition of a new society news-paper which he had named *Vanity Fair* and which was to be a weekly commentary on social and political events. Anti-radical and imperialist, its contents were up-to-date and well-informed.

One regular feature was the large lithographed caricature of a famous figure of the day. At this time Fred Burnaby could be seen striding down Pall Mall with the diminutive figure of Bowles beside him, or meeting his friend Valentine Baker at the nearby United Services Club. There was a great 'rapport' between the two cavalrymen, so alike in many ways. Both were superb horsemen, both had studied the Eastern Question at first hand, and both had tremendous courage. The main difference between them seemed to be in the single-minded devotion of Colonel Baker to his regiment, while Burnaby was influenced by a thousand other interests.

It soon became well known that the 10th Hussars were not only the smartest, but the most efficient and, incidentally, the best mounted cavalry regiment, for Valentine Baker had followed his own convictions and had concentrated on obtaining the very best horses possible, often supplying large sums from his own purse. Very soon it was said that the Regiment was 'as professional as its Commanding Officer.'

1. A family portrait. Some of Valentine's brothers and sisters. The
boys are James and John.

2. **Valentine as a young man** *(By kind permission of the late Mrs Erica Graham)*

3. **In the 12th Lancers**

4. **Sir Samuel Baker in home-made hunting kit**

5. **Lady Baker**

6. **Colonel Valentine Baker leading the 10th Hussars at a Review in the presence of HRH The Prince of Wales** *(From* Memoirs of the 10th Royal Hussars*)*

7. **Routing the robbers on the road to Amol in Persia** *(From 'Clouds in the East')*

8. **HRH The Prince of Wales**

9. **On Special Service.
Lieutenant General
Valentine Baker Pasha**

10. **Colonel Fred Burnaby of the Blues** *(From a portrait by JG Tissot in the National Portrait Gallery)*

It was during this time, and towards the end of the year, that Valentine Baker fell in love and married. His bride was Fanny, the pretty young daughter of Frank Wormald, of Potterton Hall in Yorkshire. Her uncle, Thomas Wormald, a President of the Royal College of Surgeons, also lived at Denton Park, in the same county. Fanny was extremely friendly with her cousin, another Fanny. It was a friendship that would last all their lives and prove of great importance to both Fanny and Valentine in the years ahead, when loyal friends were to prove so precious to them both. The family was also much connected with the Cavalry, and especially with the 12th Lancers, Valentine's old regiment.

Probably as a wedding present, the Prince of Wales gave the young Colonel a most beautiful and high-spirited grey, a long-tailed Arab charger. A horse which Valentine was to treasure for many years, and one which he always rode, especially on parade. An oil painting of the Prince of Wales mounted, and dressed in the uniform of the Tenth Hussars, followed by Colonel Baker on the white Arab charger, riding at the head of the Regiment, is still to be seen in the National Army Museum in London.

★ ★ ★

The next three years were memorable because of the Army manoeuvres which had now become extremely popular, and in which the cavalry took a very important part. Again, the 'Non-Pivot drill' drew spectators from home and abroad, and was, indeed, adopted by many cavalry regiments. On 19 June, 1867, the first Volunteer Review was held in the presence of Her Majesty the Queen, at Ascot, and the Regiment was inspected afterwards at Aldershot. On 11 December, the Crown Prince of Prussia, also inspected the 10th. Meanwhile, a daughter, Hermione, was born to Valentine and Fanny in 1867, a child to whom her father was to become entirely devoted. A year later, another little daughter, Sybil, arrived to complete their happiness.

There were no clouds on the horizon. The Prince of Wales honoured both brothers, Samuel and Valentine, with his warm-hearted and generous friendship, and there was nothing which could foretell the heartrending and tragic days that were to come. Valentine had chosen his bride well, for her courage, loyalty and fortitude were never to be shaken, even when the bright future became suddenly dimmed, and the world seemed at its darkest for her husband.

Meanwhile, the spirit of Army Reform was in the air. So too was the spirit of innovation – one that Valentine had never been slow to serve. In April 1869, largely in response to Valentine's strong recommendations, cavalry regiments were regrouped into four squadrons instead of the traditional eight troops. This change was not only of great tactical significance but radically affected the system of regimental administration. The idea met a good deal of opposition within the cavalry, particularly from those junior Captains for whom it meant the loss of command of their troops. The system of purchase had not yet been abolished and they feared that the change would mean a devaluation of their commissions. Nevertheless the four junior Captains of the 10th Hussars, out of loyalty to their Colonel, raised no objection. In the event, it would be only a year before Lord Cardwell's historic reforms led to the abolition of purchase.

A few weeks before the regimental reorganisation was introduced, another very significant innovation had been the introduction of military signalling throughout the Army. In consequence of this, Valentine had at once sent Cornet H.S. Gough on a signalling course at Chatham. Soon after Gough returned, Valentine introduced new signalling flags into the Regiment. On 14 July a flying column, which included the 10th Hussars, marched to Chobham, camping en route at Hampton Court, in Bushey Park. Taking advantage of this exercise, Gough soon had his signallers operating to one another across the river. Once in camp, Valentine had his new regimental flags of blue and yellow flown from every tent, with a very large one flying at the head of a tall flagpole outside the Officers' Mess.

The next day, the 10th moved on to join a vast Review on Wimbledon Common. There was a 'practice' battle, which included both the 10th Hussars and the 17th Lancers, the two regiments being brigaded under Valentine.

Perhaps the greatest Review in which the 10th were to take part took place in the following year, 1870. It was in that year that a very old officer of the 10th, Lord Thomas Cecil, who had joined the Regiment in 1816, visited them. He had been a great horseman in his day, and had taken part in the early days of steeplechasing, winning the Irish Grand Military Cup in 1832. Later, Lady Sophia Cecil, his daughter, wrote: 'The last occasion on which he saw the Tenth was at Brighton Barracks in 1870, when it was under the command of Colonel Valentine Baker, and the appearance and perfection of drill it had been brought to by that officer gave him the greatest satisfaction.'

The great Review, which was to be held at Aldershot in the presence of the Queen, was planned for 9 July. The Prince of Wales would be riding at the head of his regiment, closely escorted by Valentine. A letter from one of Valentine's sisters, Annie Bourne, describes the preparations and also her own preliminary arrangements for the Presentation of herself and Valentine's wife, Fanny, in the Queen's Drawing Room only a few days afterwards. She wrote to her little daughter:

> North Camp,
> Aldershot.

Dear Popsy,

Prince Arthur has come to the camp to do duty as a Brigade Major, and the Queen is coming over next Monday. There will be a grand Review for her of course. I am going to the Drawing Room on the 7th, after all. Yesterday I went to London for the day to choose the dress. It is to be a petticoat of pale primrose tulle, and trimmed with apple blossoms, and a tulle veil in the hair with feathers and things. . . . Think of me on Friday at 3 pm going with Aunt Fanny and a Mrs William Russell to the Drawing Room. We went yesterday to the Lord Chamberlain's office at St James' Palace to get the Presentation Cards. Mrs William Russell's husband was a Major in the 10th Hussars, Uncle Val's Regiment, but now he is Equerry to the Prince of Wales, so he will be standing behind the Prince when we are presented.

> Goodbye, darling Popsy,
> Ever your loving Mother.

★　★　★

This must have been a time of great happiness for Valentine. Fanny had been presented at Court, and he had come to be considered as one of the most brilliant soldiers of his time.

Meanwhile, for relaxation from more serious business, point-to-point races, first ridden in Ireland, were introduced to the English race-course by members of the 10th Hussars, among whom was Lord Valentia – and the first polo match was played in England in 1870 by members of the 10th Hussars and 9th Lancers.

An amusing account of the first game played between them, was written at the time:

Nearly all fashionable London journeyed from town to Hounslow on Tuesday to witness a new game, called 'Hockey on Horseback' between the officers of the 10th Prince of Wales' Hussars, and officers of the 9th Queen's Royal Lancers, who had come from Aldershot.

The game took place on Hounslow Heath and the various equipages quite surrounded the ground allotted to the players. Posts some twenty yards apart marked the goals. The distance between them a little under 200 yards. The sticks used were like those used in hockey. Both sides wore mob caps with different coloured tassels attached. The ball, a little sphere of white bone, was thrown up by a Sergeant Major of the 10th who then galloped off the ground. The eight players on each side, who had taken up position in front of the goals, then galloped for the ball at the best speed of their active, wiry little 12½ hands high ponies.

The Hussars scored three goals, and the Lancers two. Though general remarks make it evident the new game is one most fitted for cavalry soldiers, it was more remarkable for the language used by the players than anything else.

★ ★ ★

In spite of all the praise he received and success he gained in the manoeuvres, Valentine was first and foremost a serious professional soldier. When, on 17 August 1870, Major Molyneux became his second in command, Valentine felt that he could be safely left in command of the Regiment while he asked for permission to travel out as an observer in the Franco-German War. During the next two years he also had opportunities to visit foreign armies and observe their organisations and drill.

While he was away, Major Molyneux had ample opportunity to practise command of the Regiment, and when Valentine was acting as Brigadier in the subsequent manoeuvres, Molyneux again took command.

While abroad, it was not only the triumphant armies that Valentine was to visit. In his book *Clouds in the East* he mentioned seeing Benedek's army in full retreat from Konnigratz, and the beaten and tired troops crossing a 'bridge of boats' on the Danube.

Meanwhile, at home, the Queen had suffered severely from the publicity surrounding the 'Mordant Case' in 1870, which seemed again to prove to her that her son's friends were not always quite what she would wish. However, two years later, in the winter of 1872, at the same time of year as his father had developed his fatal illness twelve years before, the Prince of Wales contracted a dangerous infection, which developed into the dreaded typhoid fever.

His mother sat by his bedside throughout the crisis. His miraculous recovery added greatly to his popularity, and when, after a Thanksgiving Service, the Queen appeared beside him and even raised his hand to her lips, enthusiasm knew no bounds. The Thanksgiving Service was held on 17 February 1873, in St Paul's Cathedral, the 10th Hussars providing the escort.

The last of the three great Reviews was held in 1872, and was perhaps the most remarkable of the three.

On 2 August, Regimental Headquarters and six troops marched from Colchester to Blandford to take part in the autumn manoeuvres near Salisbury, arriving on 13 August. The strength of the Regiment at that time was 19 officers, 434 non-commissioned officers and men, with 409 horses.

The 10th formed part of the First Division of the First Army Corps, under the command of Lieutenant-General Sir John Michel GCB, the Cavalry Brigade, composed of the 7th and 10th Hussars and the 12th Lancers, being brigaded under Colonel Valentine Baker.

On 31 August the Prince of Wales himself arrived to take part in the manoeuvres, and at 10 am the 10th Hussars, with Valentine mounted on his grey charger at their head, marched into Crichel Park. The Duke and Duchess of Teck, the Prince and Princess of Saxe-Weimar, Lord Lucan, the veteran general of Crimean fame, and the Russian general Schouvanoff were among those assembled to greet the Prince. It was a proud moment for Valentine when the Prince, having made his inspection, congratulated him on finding both men and horses so fit for service.

In the evening the 10th camped in Fonthill Park and the next day a 'mimic' war was carried out between two corps of equal strength. The 10th Hussars found themselves, as we know, serving under Sir John Michel, while Sir Robert Walpole led the opposing force. It was not until September that Walpole and Michel moved to meet each other in the larger encounters of the 'mimic' war, and these manoeuvres continued until 12 September.

During these manoeuvres, all Valentine Baker's training of his regiment was shown to brilliant effect. He had given so much attention to its training in outpost and scouting duties, and to all those 'detached duties' which were amongst the roles of the cavalry, that they received the highest commendation for the energetic and intelligent manner in which all ranks worked.

'In one respect also,' the Regimental History of the 10th Hussars continues:–

. . . the 10th Hussars were especially remarkable. In purchasing re-mounts Colonel Baker had always made a point of selecting horses with as much breeding as possible, preferring to depend upon blood for hard continuous work rather than upon size and imposing appearance. The correctness of his judgment in this matter was proved by the way in which the Tenth's horses, which many people had condemned as too small and slight, sustained very severe exertions for many successive days without at all deteriorating in working power.

In the opinion of the umpires, the force under Sir John Michel was entirely successful. The manoeuvres concluded with a grand parade near Amesbury which provided a magnificent spectacle. The range of Beacon Hill, the top of which is the highest in this part of the country, partly enclosed a huge natural amphitheatre, covered with smooth turf, reaching nearly two miles in every direction. The slopes of the hill were covered with spectators, while about 30,000 soldiers, all in the highest perfection of equipment and military skill, were gathered in the level space. It was a glorious, sunny day.

After the usual inspection and march past, the cavalry formed into two lines which charged in succession to the saluting position and 'nothing more splendidly striking' could be seen than the rapid advance of these divisions each composed of six Regiments.

★   ★   ★

The Autumn Manoeuvres of 1872 were the last great military exercise in which the 10th Hussars were to take part, for instructions came though in November for them to prepare for embarkation for service once again in India.

After much heart-searching and sadness, Valentine now decided that it would be right, after thirteen years' service in command of the Regiment, for him to make way for a younger man. He wrote: 'After thirteen years' command of the 10th Hussars, the period had arrived when a tie so long maintained and which I can only compare to the love of a father for his children, must be snapped and broken. . .'

The whole Regiment was sad to see him go. On 21 December the Prince of Wales honoured the officers of the Regiment by inviting them to dinner at Marlborough House. Valentine was to be succeeded by Major the Hon. C.C. Molyneux and Captain Ralph Kerr was appointed second-in-command. Lieutenant Viscount Valentia, who had so often ridden in the regimental steeplechases, retired at the same time as his Colonel.

Perhaps the most fitting tribute to Valentine, was made in the Regimental History, written by one of the officers who knew him well. Colonel Liddell, who was afterwards to command the Regiment, wrote:

> As a commanding officer and military instructor he was able to invest the dry details of drill with the highest interest, and in his time it was a common remark among the subalterns of the Tenth that a Colonel's field-day was as good fun as a day's hunting. He had the power of expressing himself most forcibly, simply and distinctly, either in speaking or writing, and no-one could ever be in his company without being impressed with the clearness and vigour of his mind. Generous, brave and kind-hearted, he left a reputation in the 10th Hussars which will not soon be forgotten.

8

CLOUDS IN THE EAST

Lieutenant-Colonel Molyneux was to prove a very worthy successor to Valentine Baker in the difficulties and dangers which were to beset the Regiment in India. He was later to be followed by Lord Ralph Kerr. The Regiment took an active part in escorting the Prince of Wales on his visit to India and later fought in the Second Afghan War.

It was after this campaign that Sir Sam Browne wrote of the 10th Hussars in August 1879:

> The Regiment is one that any Service in the world would be proud of. Tried in the field at Futtehabad against greatly superior numbers, tested in many and long days of reconnaissance, and outpost duty, in the accident at the ford of the Kabul river, and in the attack of cholera while passing through the Khyber, the high discipline and soldier-like qualities of this noble Regiment have ever shone forth, proving no less the efficiency of the present officers than the careful training it has received in the past.

It was a very real tribute to Valentine. Meanwhile, in his own words, he said modestly: 'I knew that some little time must elapse before any fresh military appointment would claim my services. I determined to devote this interval to useful purpose, to endeavour to penetrate the mystery which hung over those Eastern deserts, and to bring back, if possible, political, geographical and strategical information that might be valuable.'

It had been many years since Valentine had had any real holiday. In his short periods of leave he had shot with his brother, and his many regimental friends, he had been part of the lighthearted London Society which surrounded the Prince of Wales, but, as we have seen, he had only been abroad on duty, or as a military observer in the Franco-

German War – and for five or six years he had been stationed in Ireland. Now, at last, the opportunities seemed limitless. He could travel in Turkey, Persia and beyond, in his own time, he could fulfil the dream of the three young brothers so long ago at Scutari, and ride through the Caucasus, evaluating for himself the power of Russia, and her expansion towards Herat and Afghanistan. He could see for himself how far she had progressed towards the boundary of the Oxus River.

It was a time when this expedition would prove very popular. For only a few years before, in 1868, alarmed at the gradual expansionist policy of Russia, Gladstone had sent a mission to St Petersburg, suggesting that the river Oxus should become Russia's southern frontier. The Russians had replied by sending one of their most charming diplomats to London, who explained that only a few companies and a few Cossacks were to be employed, in an entirely humanitarian venture, to release some of their countrymen who were held prisoner, and without the slightest idea of an extension of territory. This satisfied the Government temporarily, but, as Valentine wrote: 'In the minds of those who were responsible for the strategic knowledge of the countries in question, the subject . . . did not die away so easily. It had been discovered that we were in a lamentable state of ignorance relative to the geography of the region which lies south of the Amoo Darya.'

He therefore determined to set out, partly on a much-needed holiday, and partly to discover for himself the extent of Russia's dominance, whilst also riding over the North Persian frontier, from Sarakhs to the Caspian Sea, which had never been entirely explored.

In this passion for exploration Valentine was very like his elder brother, Sam, who just before Valentine set off, had been welcomed at Khartoum on his return from his second great expedition to Africa. On this expedition he had attempted to put down the cruel slave trade. He had been away for three years and for at least two years had been given up for lost, with his beautiful wife, Florence. Valentine took two companions with him – a Lieutenant Gill of the Royal Engineers, who would complete the journey with him and prove a very loyal and faithful friend, and Captain Clayton of the 9th Lancers, who would develop cholera when they reached Tehran and have to be invalided home.

As was usual in those days, Valentine took an enormous quantity of supplies. In fact, at Charing Cross Station it was discovered that their baggage weighed more than a ton. They not only took a wide variety of guns, but also uniforms to wear on special occasions, fishing tackle, a rubber dinghy for duck shooting, a medicine chest containing Leiburg insect powder (which proved quite useless), Whitehead's cakes of soap, quinine and a variety of other medicines, and an enormous supply of food. The question of carrying their baggage did not really arise, as it was almost always possible to hire mules and porters for transport.

Valentine was to take a double-barrelled rifle by Laing, a Westley-Richard's express, 'My old shoulder single-barrelled duck gun No. 4 which carried a ball beautifully up to 80 yards, and with 8 drachms of powder could be a most formidable weapon for tigers, a double-barrelled No. 12 Purdey gun and also a revolver of a very large bore by Holland, somewhat heavy, the barrel and all the works silvered with nickel (to prevent rust).'

At length they set off, sailing down the Danube, as Sam had so many years before, passing Widdin and so on to Constantinople.

Memories of the Crimean War flooded back, as Valentine visited Scutari, but, he wrote that it had been so enlarged that he 'scarcely found the old house looking over the Bosphorus, in which I had lived for some months after the War'.

Their first objective was to reach Tiflis, where Prince Michael of Russia was to prove a very real friend to the small party. For the Prince of Wales, having heard of the purposed journey, graciously lent them all the aid in his power, giving Valentine letters to the Grand Duke Michael which proved invaluable in forwarding the success of the expedition.

On their arrival at Tiflis, on the Russian border, however, he learnt that the Prince had left for London. So Valentine called on Prince Mirsky with his letters of introduction. Prince Mirsky was Prince Michael's second-in-command and he could not have been more helpful. The small party was royally entertained not only socially, but was also encouraged to see the arsenal, the military hospital, and to visit the School of Military Instruction. Prince Mirsky had himself fought in the Crimea, and had been wounded at the battle of Tchernaya. It was impossible for him not to discuss his memories with another equally distinguished soldier, and he also ordered his aide-de-camp to show Valentine everything of military interest.

Valentine dined with Prince Mirsky and with Colonel Tolstoy, going to the Opera in the evening, and strolling in the famous Sans Souci Gardens. Here he met ladies 'of the higher classes', but noted that he saw 'Pretty faces, but not in as large a proportion as would be found in any English ballroom'.

It was a fascinating three weeks, but on the return of Prince Michael, and armed with the letters he had given them, Valentine and his friends determined to start their expedition to Tehran. At first they travelled by

Barouche, their servants in a Troika, or cart filled with hay, in which they lay while travelling at high speed – but horses were soon engaged. They were escorted by Cossacks, who had military settlements along the frontier, and who galloped around them doing amazing feats on horseback.

Valentine had asked for permission from Prince Michael to visit Tchikishlar and the Attreck. Permission had been granted, and they had dined at the Palace before setting off, after attending a magnificent review of the whole Garrison.

Although he had admired the troops' power of endurance, even in this spectacular review Valentine Baker had found their movements far too slow. The review, and the farewell dinner which followed, meant that they set off after midnight for Tehran.

Before leaving, they were warned of bandits, who might attack them on the way, but Valentine would only take six men instead of twelve, as escorts. He wrote: 'It would have been hard, indeed, if we three Englishmen, all armed with revolvers, and with guns and rifles quite handy and ready, could not have held our own against any such desultory attack.'

They reached Enzelli, the port for Tehran on the Caspian Sea, without incident, but heard from a Russian general that the Russian advance on Khiva had failed, and that 120 horses had died. They were refused any transport to the Attreck river, and realised that their journey to the Attreck and Tchikishlar was rather unpopular, as every sort of excuse was made to prevent their journey. They stayed with the Russian Consul at Astrabad but were soon on their way to Tehran.

It was here that they really began to enjoy their holiday in Persia. The walled city, with its flat-roofed houses and fortifications, stood out against a backdrop of snow-covered blue mountains. The Shah himself was away in Europe but they soon formed a friendship with a Mr Thompson and Dr Baker from the Embassy. Valentine decided that during the hot season it would be better to travel in the mountains, shooting and fishing, until the autumn came and the long journey from Sharood to Meshed could be attempted, across what was virtually a sandy waste, too hot and stifling in the summer months to be attempted.

Just as Sam compared his various guns, so Valentine wrote that, for larger animals, 'My advice would be to use as large a calibre as you can manage comfortably, without suffering too much from the recoil . . . I shall always remember with respect the marvellous effect produced in our elephant hunting excursions in Ceylon by the ponderous weapons which my brother, Sir Samuel Baker, generally used – but not one man in a thousand could have managed them. I shall not easily forget . . . the result when, in a desperate chase, a gun-bearer by mistake handed me his spare rifle instead of mine, and when I fired both the elephant and myself were prostrated at the same moment!'

He also said he did not believe in 'long shots' of 200–300 yards. He wrote: 'It has been my lot to shoot with some of the best sportsmen and best rifle shots in the world, and I have never seen this accuracy. On the contrary, when these long shots have to be taken, a number of animals go off wounded, and there is nothing so distressing to a true sportsman as this, to cause unnecessary and useless suffering.'

Valentine was delighted with the ponies which he found he could purchase in Tehran, sturdy and immensely courageous, they were in fine condition. He purchased a small grey for himself, which he nick-named 'Cremorne', after the famous racehorse, and his friend bought a gallant black pony, whilst a third pony was purchased and named 'Macaroni'. He ventured into the bazaars in Tehran and found magnificent carpets, but they were not for the traveller, all the more valuable ones being for the Persians themselves. He found that in their houses they would spread the most precious carpets, for there was no other furniture, and the most distinguished guest would be invited to sit upon the most valuable carpet, while those not so distinguished would be placed on one of lesser value.

Valentine was horrified at the condition of his supplies on arrival at the capital. The jolting road from Tiflis to Tehran had resulted in 'the most disastrous results. Baking powder and Lieburg insect powder, and Worcester sauce, tea and broken bottles were all mixed up together in a compound impossible to describe.' When this was eventually sorted out, he himself went down with fever, but was cured by Dr Baker. The third member of the party had become seriously ill with cholera and had to leave the expedition, but Valentine and Lieutenant Gill prepared to set out on their journey.

At last all was ready, and their party set off, shooting Moufflon and fishing the river Lar in the north. The mountain paths were so steep that it was miraculous that the ponies kept to the them. On one occasion Cremorne had thrown a shoe, just as Valentine had reached a peak from which their tent was visible, far below. He wrote:

> There was a narrow zigzag path which led down to the nearly perpendicular side of the mountain and, as it was so narrow, it was awkward to lead the pony. I let him go, and drove him before me. We had descended nearly half way, and had come to a part where the mountain was a little less steep,

when Cremorne suddenly left the zigzag and walked like a goat along the most precipitous side of the hill. I thought every moment he must roll to the bottom, but he scrambled on for about ten yards, and then stood quietly munching some herbs that grew from the rocks . . . I tried coaxing but it was useless, Cremorne looked at me stolidly, but moved not. The situation was so absurd that I burst out laughing.

Luckily he finally managed to catch the pony, but this little incident shows the light-hearted way in which Valentine was enjoying his freedom from responsibility in the beautiful mountain scenery with which he was surrounded.

They managed to shoot ibex, despite the fact that Valentine found the beasts disturbed by one of his horse keepers, who, leading Cremorne, was actually singing! The fishing was amazingly good, and the trout caught in the river Lar excellent. Valentine wrote: 'Tell me if you ever ate a fish to compare with a Lar trout that only an hour before was in his native stream! What pleasant days we passed by the side of that beautiful river!'

Finally, on 12 August, they felt they must move on to Shahrood, and set off, riding about thirty miles a day. It was on this road that they had their first encounter with bandits. One of the tent-pitchers was set upon and severely beaten up, and, as they pressed on to report the incident to the Governor of the province, at a town named Amol, the baggage and mules which followed them were set upon by a large gang. Valentine and Shaab immediately sprang on their ponies and galloped back, for their money and spare fire-arms and ammunition were among the stores. They found their big India tent thrown into a pool, and two muleteers lying on the ground, groaning. Their chief servant, Gerome, had most sensibly formed a sort of breastwork of the baggage, and when Valentine arrived he found him with the rest of the servants, ready to fire whenever the attacking party, which completely surrounded them, appeared from the high grass.

The road was also blocked by about twenty men. Valentine wrote 'Trusting to the effect of a sudden initiative, and calling to Shaab and Gerome to follow, we dashed straight at the party blocking the Amol road. No sooner did these men find we were going to attack than they broke in all directions, running for their lives over the deepest bogs, and clambering over the fences of the rice fields.' Valentine then charged the main body, and they also fled, but must have been horrified to find themselves hotly pursued. They had quite misjudged the travellers they were about to attack, who were far from fearful merchants. They found

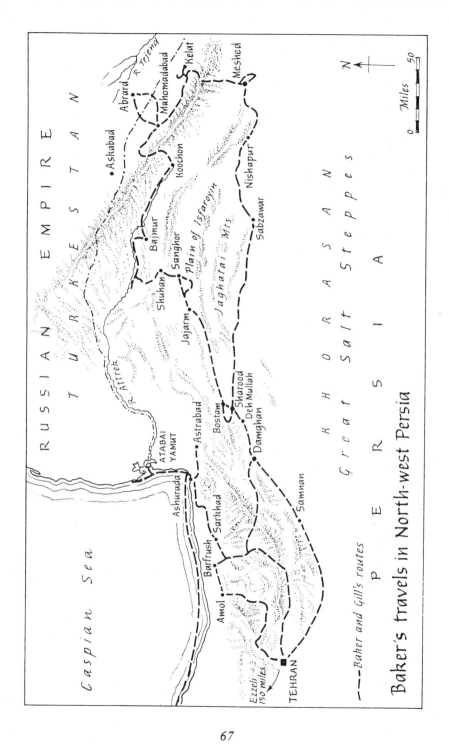

Baker's travels in North-west Persia

--- Baker and Gill's routes

Caspian Sea

RUSSIAN EMPIRE

T U R K E S T A N

• Askabad

Abrard

Mahomadabad

Kelat

Meshed

Koochon

Bajmur

Sanghor

Nishapur

Shuhan

Plain of Isfaroyin

Jaghatai Mtrs.

Sabzawar

Jajarm

K H O R A S A N

Great Salt Steppes

P E R S I A

Ashurada

ATABAI
YAMUT

R. Attrek

R. Tejend

Astrabad

Bostam

Sharood

Deh Mullah

Damghan

Barfrush

Sarkhad

Amol

Samnan

Ezzeli
150 miles

TEHRAN

N

Miles

0   50

67

themselves instead at the mercy of a Colonel of the 10th Hussars. He wrote:

> Meanwhile the ringleaders had been going like greyhounds and were well ahead again. One man, who had been very prominent, was beginning to slacken. I took the little grey tight by the head and drove him through the deep mud, as fast as he could go. The man saw I was gaining rapidly . . . In another minute the muzzle of a gun was at his head and he was a prisoner. And a most troublesome prisoner he proved, for, although at one moment he would beg for mercy, the next instant he would be shouting to his comrades who had reached the village to come to his rescue, and he positively refused to move when we urged him to do so. Pointing the gun at him was of no use. He seemed to know perfectly well that I should not shoot him. We tried to tie his hands, but this he would not allow: and we felt ridiculously powerless, for I did not want to hurt him.
>
> There was no help for it. The only way was to get rid of one's arms and meet him on equal terms. He was a powerful muscular man; so, as I was bigger than G–, I gave him my gun and pistol, and then closed with our captive; and it was not without a severe struggle that I threw him and secured his hands with my handkerchief.

At length they led him and two other prisoners back and they confessed to having taken part in a plot to rob the travellers. Shaab was put in charge of the prisoners, but Valentine wrote:

> 'In the morning there was a sudden alarm. Shaab had gone to sleep; the guard had followed suit; and the prisoners were off. Abbas came and spoke to me reproachfully; in fact, it was a little my fault. The evening before, he had secured the captives with ropes. Hearing some groaning I went out and found that he had tied them so tightly that it would be positive torture for men to remain thus bound all night; and I ordered the cords to be slackened, and the prisoners carefully watched. The result was that they were all off. How is it that no men of Eastern race ever make efficient sentries? Had I an Asiatic army as an enemy, I would always attack an hour before daybreak. Their sentries would be certain to be asleep, and their men unprepared. We marched off, rather crestfallen, at the escape of our prisoners.'

A little later on they were attacked again. This time Valentine realised that it was because of religious prejudice and because it was the first time Europeans had travelled through that part of the country. He wrote:

> Matters were looking serious, they had poured in showers of large stones to good effect. I had been twice hit on the head, but my pith hat saved me

> ... being most anxious that the English name should not be associated with violence and bloodshed, except in case of dire necessity, I had given strict orders not to fire without my command. . . . But there is a limit to forbearance, and I was determined that they should not stop us. Never halt or retreat in face of an Eastern enemy, it is always fatal.

He rode forward and talked to the bandits. It worked like magic. Their guns were confiscated while Valentine told them 'of the danger of stopping Englishmen in this forcible manner, and, on their clearing the road, and apologising, restored their guns'.

At length, after these quite alarming episodes, so calmly dealt with by the party, they passed the minarets of Damghan and reached Shahrood and Bostam. Here they rested their horses, in preparation for the long and weary march across the desert to Meshed.

Shahrood, Valentine noted, was at an important junction of the road from East to West, and from this point he was to concentrate on the military aspects of the journey, and in particular on the relations of Persia and her northern neighbour, and the expansion of Russia towards Afghanistan.

The Governor of Bostam suggested that as a large 'caravan' was en route for Meshed, he would be very glad if Valentine could join it and command 'the escort'. To this Valentine agreed, but wrote, 'Irregular they were indeed. They were the wildest troops possible, mostly Tartars.' He still rode his favourite pony, Cremorne, and they set off along the long and dusty road in procession, passing the famous turquoise mines on the way. By now, Valentine himself was suffering from dysentery and only his sense of duty carried him on. 'We decided,' he wrote, 'to enter Meshed in uniform,' and for this occasion he rode a 'richly caparisoned Arab horse.'

The great mosque of Imam Resa came in sight with its gilded dome and they were glad to arrive safely after the long journey. Here they met Abbas Khan, the Persian representative from Tehran, and Valentine had a long talk with the Governor, who said that the Russians were already encroaching on Persian land. Abbas Khan recommended an excellent Persian medicine for dysentery, a tea similar to linseed tea with the addition of a teaspoonful of sweet almonds. It was miraculous and once more Valentine could consider continuing his journey. He was now in the very heart of Persia.

They visited a fine old Persian Prince who possessed a wonderful collection of treasures, and Valentine was able to buy a beautiful grey horse, a Turkoman, which he eventually brought back to England. But there was one great disappointment, they had to give up all hope of going to Afghanistan and Herat, as Yakoub Khan, the Governor sent a letter saying that he had 'most positive instructions' not to receive them unless they came with an order from the British Government. No letter had been received from Lord Northbrook in answer to Valentine's request and so, very regretfully, he decided instead to travel northwards to Kelat. Before leaving Meshed, he noted how guns and artillery could be easily brought along the road to Herat, and wrote 'Mountains do not necessarily make a barrier – those who hold the passes are in control' and he noted how Nadir Shah had marched on India through Afghanistan 136 years before, and had captured Delhi. He considered Herat the key to India for Herat itself is only 540 miles from Quetta.

He wrote: 'It is true that when war broke out with Russia [the Crimean War] Russia could not think of invading Afghanistan, but the counter-move was planned, and we know of what it consisted. Intrigues were put on foot, which may even have influenced India at the time of the Mutiny.'

At length the small party left Meshed to climb through mountainous country to Kelat. The road became a narrow gorge, but at length they came out on a beautiful mountain side covered with juniper trees. There was a serious mutiny among the servants who had joined the party to go to Meshed, and, now, fearing raids by the Turkomans, refused to go further. They were summarily dealt with, and at length Valentine and his friend reached Kelat, a gigantic natural fortress. Here Valentine managed to save the lives of some unfortunate Turkoman prisoners, by appealing to the Governor for leniency. He not only saved them from death, but gave them money to return to their own homes.

He was sure that the mountains around them were the true frontier of North West Persia and wrote:

> I sat for nearly an hour on that mountain top in a dreamy reverie. The immense future political importance of the scene which lay at my feet gave it an almost painful and absorbing interest. That great background of mountains, one felt, was the true old frontier of North-West Persia, and there to the East again, I saw it running on, and knew that I was looking at Afghanistan with all its wild and thrilling memories. Then, when my mind wandered to the great political problems of the future, and of British and Russian notes, and imagining difficulties in defining frontier boundaries in these regions, the whole thing seemed a farce, for Nature had dawn a line more clearly than the hand of man could ever fashion it. These giant mountains formed the outer wall, Tejend and Merv the advance posts; beyond,

the sea of desert right away to the Oxus. If Russia had the Oxus, and a line were drawn between it and Merv, what better boundary could be found?

He was interrupted in his reverie by his Khourd guide who showed him the line of old forts at the base of the hills, and also gave him an account of a famous Turkoman horse that had been captured some time before from a Turkoman chief. This news immediately riveted Valentine's attention, and the political situation was momentarily forgotten, for Turkoman horses were famous in Persia. Not only were they equal in beauty to an English race-horse but they were immensely powerful. Valentine immediately asked to see him. He was a perfect type of Turkoman, and through the good offices of Abbas Khan, he immediately purchased him, at length taking him home to England, where he hoped he would be of the greatest value in giving 'a streak of extraordinary stoutness' to the thoroughbred stock at home.

Valentine was immensely interested in the wild Turkoman tribesmen. They lived on the borders of Persia between Khiva, Savakhs, the Oxus and the North Persian frontier. The men wore a long brown dress, with the fur inside, similar to that worn by the Afghans, and a fur cap. Their diet was frugal, a mere handful of millet and milk, but violent robbery was considered by them the highest of virtues, notwithstanding their 'Sunni' faith. Their only saving grace was their great love for their horses. Valentine wrote: 'And well do these noble animals deserve all the care that is lavished upon them, for in courage, speed and endurance combined, they stand at the head of the equine race.'

It was said that Tamerlane had originally brought 14,000 of the best Arab mares into the country, and that the Turkoman horses were their direct descendants.

In his book *Clouds in the East*, Valentine describes a raid by the Turkomans, on a Persian village. First, their horses would be brought, by special diet and exercise, to such a pitch of condition that they could gallop many miles without rest. The village would be settled upon, and the horses would then swoop down upon the unfortunate villagers. The women would be carried off and the men tied behind the horses. No pity was shown to the stragglers and the village would usually be burnt. The raids took place all along the frontier with Persia, the Persians being quite unable to defend themselves. They too had little to recommend them, for they lived mainly by extortion and corruption at that time.

Valentine was constantly warned of an attack on his party by the Turkomans, but whether it was because he was well-armed, or because he had shown pity on the Turkoman prisoners, he was never molested in any way.

After travelling to Kelat, they made their way by swift stages to the Attreck, as Valentine was determined to discover its true source, and actually traced it to Kara Kazan, passing through Mahomedabad and Koochon.

At Mahomedabad Valentine saw another magnificent Turkoman horse, tethered in the Governor's courtyard, at least 17 hands high. This horse was given to him by the Governor, and was taken back to England with the one he had bought. Finally, following the road from Sanghor to Jajarm the party reached Shahrood once more, to be told that the steamer on the Caspian Sea would be leaving in only a few days' time.

The journey to Tehran was a tremendous effort, and meant riding almost sixty miles a day. At last, completely exhausted, they rode up to the gates late one evening. By this time Valentine was prostrated with fever, but the gatekeeper kept them waiting for several hours while their papers were checked, only passing some wood through to them so that they could light a fire to warm themselves. At last the gates were opened, a search for the Legation was successful and Dr Baker was woken up at 3 am by some desperately tired and weary travellers. He showed no surprise or anger and Valentine very soon found himself in a comfortable bed, being well cared for. But they could not stay long, if they were to catch the boat, and as soon as he was well enough to move, Valentine was sent on with his good friend Lieutenant Gill to join the ship at Enzelli, the Persian port on the Caspian.

Cremorne had been given to one of Valentine's faithful guides, the Turkoman horses being sent on to England as planned. As he stood on the deck of the *Constantine* he looked back. He wrote:

> Nothing could exceed the beauty of the view from the deck of the steamer. Enzelli lay in the foreground on a narrow strip of land, picturesque and well-wooded; and the backwater of Enzelli stretched beyond like a vast lake, whilst the bend in the Caspian towards the north, formed a semi-circle of lofty mountains . . . whose bases were covered with forest and exhibited the beautiful autumn tints, their rugged peaks being all white with snow. We said goodbye to our kind host Captain Abbott; the paddle wheels revolved slowly, and we were off. As we gazed at the lovely view before us, we bade farewell to Persia.

All through that adventurous holiday, Valentine had shown the characteristics which had so endeared him to his regiment. His complete disregard of physical hardship and of danger when threatened by bandits, his humanity in dealing with his prisoners which, although it led to their escape, was very similar to the generosity he had shown to the wild Irish subaltern, O'Reilly, when he was to have been executed (see page 49). His kindness to the condemned Turkoman prisoners, when he actually gave them money to return to their own homes, showed a sympathy in his nature which was particularly striking in the age in which he lived. His devotion to the Turkoman horses of course went without question, and he was proud to be returning home to England with at least two of that magnificent breed.

★   ★   ★

On his return from Persia, Valentine learned that he had been appointed Assistant Quartermaster General at Aldershot. It was a Colonel's post, newly created at the time of the Cardwell reforms. He was due to assume it in the autumn of 1874.

After a great welcome home, he found that he was very much in demand, not only in the drawing-rooms of society, and among members of the dashing Marlborough Club, but as a serious lecturer and writer on the problems of the Middle East.

On 8 May, 1874, he gave an illustrated lecture to the United Services Institute in London. He gave as its title, 'The Military Geography of Central Asia' and spoke on the subject of Russian expansion with statesmanlike moderation. He said:

> We aim at no extension of our territory to the East, but simply seek to make all due provision for the safety of our Indian Empire, and for the proper protection of its trade and commerce . . . I have endeavoured to show that it is better both for the interests of Russia and England that a broad and distinct line of demarcation should exist between their possessions.
>
> We have only to look back to the events within the living memory of almost all in this room, to see how much there is to lament in the past. How many must there be present who served in the Crimean War? Do not those who then served look back with pardonable pride to all the deeds of gallantry and daring which were done in that hard and trying campaign and siege? And do not gentler thoughts come back of comrades gone from us, and what is more, lost for England for ever? But what should we have thought, that all for which they suffered and fought to conquer, be thrown to the winds by the actions of Diplomacy in a few short years?

Russian expansion was still the problem of the hour, and Valentine's brother, James, set off himself on a similar expedition to Persia on a fact-finding expedition during 1875–6. Perhaps inspired by the brothers, Fred Burnaby, Valentine's popular and powerful friend, was also to travel to Khiva on his magnificent and historic 'ride' – a ride which was to make him famous, for no other Englishman had been allowed to approach the city, which was almost unknown.

He rode, as Valentine had ridden, an average of fifty or sixty miles a day, at last reaching Khiva, and finding that Russian troops had indeed occupied that magical and oriental city. But Burnaby was recalled by the Commander-in-Chief, the Duke of Cambridge, almost at once. He did not think it was the duty of members of the Household Cavalry to show such a spirit of independence.

Meanwhile, Valentine had been settling into his new appointment and writing his book, *Clouds in the East*, about his adventurous journey and describing the situation in Central Asia as he now saw it. The book, which was published in 1875, contains a very warm tribute to the assistance that he had received from Prince Michael and Prince Mirsky, whose letters of introduction had made so much possible for him.

Only in the Appendix did he bring his 'great guns' to bear upon the military situation. Accepting that the Russians were ever extending their influence over the Caucasus, he first showed their complete dominance over the ports of the Caspian Sea. The most viable port, Ashourada, was in Russian hands, and the only one open to the Persians was Enzelli: in fact, since the Russians had signed the Treaty of Turkmantchi in 1828, they had turned the Caspian Sea into 'a purely Russian lake'.

Ashourada was the principal naval station on the Caspian and, whilst Valentine was staying at Astrabad, he had also made a short expedition to the Atteck and Gourgan rivers – he had seen then that Russia, although nominally only in possession of the Attreck, had quietly taken possession of both banks of the Gourgan, thus effectively denying the Persians that valuable access to the Caspian Sea. This gradual expansion had at length led to the occupation of Khiva in 1873, by the forces of General Kauffman, and from Khiva it would seem that the next step might be Russian expansion to Merv and Herat, a route which represented the gateway to Afghanistan and so possibly to India.

Valentine had been refused a pass to Khiva, and in spite of all his hopes, he had been firmly denied access to Herat. It seemed to him that the Persian government was almost as blind as the British to this slow Russian advance, and seemed quite unaware of their plans for the extension of the railways.

Valentine felt that the grand opening of the new railway by Baron Reuter, which he had witnessed, might mean a tremendous change in the facility of transporting troops from one area to another in the case of hostilities. He emphasised that Russian railways were projected not from commercial, but strategic, considerations and that his own country, if it did not take the opportunity to pre-empt the situation, would find that the Russian railways would dominate both Turkey and Persia. It is interesting to note that de Lesseps had actually put forward a plan for the railways but it had not been accepted.

He finally put forward five proposals for action by his own country:

1. A bolder policy
2. The establishment of a desert boundary north of Persia and Afghanistan by a Russian and English Commission
3. The development of railways and the extension of trade in those countries which lie on our side of this boundary, gauge being especially considered
4. The reorganisation of the Indian Army
5. The occupation of Quetta
6. The settlement of the Afghan succession and the opening up of Afghanistan by railways to trade
7. The supply of horses to India drawn from the Teke Turkomans
8. The settlement of the Merv difficulty
9. That Persia should be urged to occupy and hold her proper Northern frontier

It is a measure of Valentine's grasp of strategy and international affairs that, just one hundred years later, his vision of the future had become true and the Soviet Union had marched into Afghanistan, albeit with the support of an air force that no soldier of Valentine's generation could possibly have imagined, just as he had predicted.

9

'A MOMENT OF MADNESS'

It is easy to understand how the dashing young Colonel must have felt that the world was at his feet in the summer of 1875; back from an unforgettable holiday, recovered from his illness and holding an important new appointment. Recognised as the Army's leading expert on cavalry doctrine, a successful author and accepted authority on 'Eastern' affairs, he was a personal friend of the Heir to the Throne and fêted in London society – most important of all, to him, he was happily married with two lovely daughters who he adored. Now, on 28 August, a splendid Review, followed by manoeuvres, was to be held at Aldershot and who could have been better qualified or more enthusiastic to organise it all than he?

The Review was to be in honour of His Highness Seyed bin Saed, the Sultan of Zanzibar, who was arriving on a State visit. The Prince and Princess of Wales and the Commander-in-Chief, His Royal Highness, the Duke of Cambridge, were to be present. So too was the beautiful Empress Eugénie of France, now living in exile in England, and who had already met his brother, Sam, at the opening of the Suez Canal.

The afternoon of 17 May was hot and sunny – it seemed almost a crime to be travelling by train that day, and not riding his famous grey Arab in the Park. He had been staying at Almond's Hotel in London the night before, and had only come down for the day to organise the manoeuvres and was now about to return. The train, with carriages still so like the elegant horse-drawn carriages of an earlier date, was waiting at Liphook Station when he arrived.

In those days, the six-wheeled first class carriages were entirely constructed of teak, as, because of its oily nature, it was supposed to defy the vagaries of the English climate. Each was divided into three compartments, entirely separated from each other, with no communicating door. There were comfortable buttoned leather seats, rich tapestry and mahogany furnishings, and elegant Holland roller blinds for the windows. Valentine entered the train very light-heartedly for he had no baggage and only wished to return to London in order to dine that night with the Duke of Cambridge.

The step outside the carriage was high and wide, the window could be opened with an embossed leather strap, and, as was perhaps the custom (although it seemed unknown to Valentine), the top-hatted guard had previously locked the other door at Guildford, so that only one door could open on the platform side. Whether this was for safety, one can only guess.

In those days there was no communication cord, but a bell, situated in the centre of the carriage, which could be rung in case of any emergency and was connected to the guard's compartment further down the train.

One can imagine Valentine's surprise, when he found there was already another passenger in the compartment – a young and very attractive young lady, dressed in the fashion of the day, with tight waist, a 'bustle' and an attractive little hat. Her 'box', or trunk, tightly strapped, was already in the compartment. She was unchaperoned. In those early days of rail travel it was not at all usual for young ladies to travel alone without a companion, relation or maid. However, she seemed to him attractive, charming and all that a young lady should be, and when he offered to close the window in case of a draught, she smiled charmingly and said that she enjoyed the light breeze. He looked forward, with surprise, to a delightful journey.

It is on record that her two sisters and a maid had 'seen her off' at Midhurst Station, and she had managed to change trains successfully alone at Liphook. She was to confide to the Colonel that she was travelling to London on the first part of a journey for a holiday in Switzerland which had been arranged for her. She was to go to her doctor brother's house on arrival in London, in Chesterfield Street. She also told him of another brother serving at Aldershot in the Army and a third brother, a barrister. From her pretty hat to her gloved hands, she was ready, she felt, for her exciting holiday, but no doubt the preparations, the packing and the general commotion of departure had tired her, and with nerves on edge, she had not felt quite at ease when the door flew open and the powerful Colonel, in civilian dress, had stepped in.

Nervously, feeling the lack of any sort of chaperone, she decided to talk brightly and gaily to him, during the journey hoping that she appeared more sophisticated than was really the case.

To Valentine, this young and charming companion seemed at first a delightful diversion on a somewhat dull and prosaic journey. As the carriage swayed along, and the spring blossom and green summer fields flew past the windows, he became more and more attracted to her pretty face and charming gestures.

At Woking Station the train halted, but there was to be no other stop until Clapham Junction.

As a founder member of the Prince of Wales's sophisticated Marlborough Club, Valentine belonged to a set of light hearted men, full of life, who delighted in unconventional behaviour and in flouting the rather stuffy decorum of Victorian society. Understandably, perhaps, it was a club of which the Queen did not entirely approve. Nevertheless, it was one to which all the Prince's closest friends belonged.

Valentine, whose devotion to duty and whose brilliance as a soldier were unquestioned, had become accustomed to relax in this rather unconventional atmosphere, and so, in the train, on that bright May day, he perhaps mistook his young companion, who had been brought up quietly with her sisters in the country, for one of the more sophisticated young ladies whom he was accustomed to meet in London.

From the time the train left Woking, we have only her statement in the witness-box to describe what actually happened, for Valentine positively refused to comment on that statement or to accuse her in any way.*

She said that he asked her whether she normally travelled alone. To this she answered with asperity 'Never'.

It would not have been really surprising if he became momentarily carried away by his own feelings – she said that he crossed over to her side of the carriage, pulled up the window, and took her hand, and begged her to give him a kiss. Lighthearted though this might seem to him, to her, brought up in the country, and suddenly realising that she was alone, locked into the compartment, with no hope of escape, with a powerful stranger, the whole thing seemed suddenly terrifying. She remembered, too late, her mother's warnings, never to talk to strangers, especially in railway trains. She did not appeal to his better nature but felt a sudden panic. The hot compartment seemed unbearably close – her tightly-laced waist unbearably constricting, and here, beside her, was a tremendously tall and terrifying stranger, asking if he might kiss

*The description of the journey is taken from Miss Dickinson's statement in Court, reported in *The Times* on 3 August 1875.

her. She sprang up and flung herself towards the emergency bell, which she pressed feverishly.

In doing so, all her claims to sophistication had vanished. No doubt Valentine made some attempt to restrain her, perhaps seizing her hand, but this is not on record. It is however recorded that the emergency bell failed to work. There was no slowing down of the train, no kind guard appearing at the window. Miss Dickinson said that the Colonel repeatedly kissed her, and it was then that she began to scream. It was the Victorian woman's strongest weapon, as many anxious fathers and brothers knew only too well, and once she started to scream, she could not stop.

Valentine must have been astonished, and his astonishment turned to the most acute and terrible anxiety as she rushed to the window, let down the strap and screamed loudly – so loudly, that two rather conventional young men, who were travelling in the next compartment, a Mr Pike and a Mr Burnett, put their heads out of the window to see what could have happened.

To their astonishment they saw a wild and distraught young lady, whose hat had by now suddenly blown away and whose hair was streaming in the wind, asking them when the train would next stop. Thoroughly disturbed, but seeing the young lady apparently well and only hysterical, they replied rather primly 'We do not know' and withdrew from the window.

Now the situation became even more frightful for the Colonel. For the little hat, so carefully chosen and so deliciously perched upon her head at the start of the journey, was gone. And in those Victorian days, to lose one's hat or to go out without a hat, was considered quite 'impossible'. As one lady of a generation later remarked, 'If one saw a lady without a hat out of doors, one would think that her house must be on fire, or something like that.'

Now, Miss Dickinson found her whole day had been ruined for her. Her pretty hat, on which she had spent so much time, had blown away. All her preparations for her holiday had been spoilt. She screamed even more loudly, with her back against the door, while Valentine begged her to stop. It was useless, impossible to reason with her. She was beyond reason.

One can only imagine the shock, the self-condemnation, the horror of the situation which became apparent to the other member of the carriage. Valentine was used to managing men and horses, but he had had no experience of hysterical girls. Nothing he could say or do was of any use.

On they sped through the peaceful countryside, and the whole situation became a nightmare to the Colonel. Suddenly, quite horrifyingly, he saw her left hand was on the door latch and in another moment she was falling backwards, out of the carriage – he sprang forward – in a moment he had seized her wrist. In falling, she said in evidence later, she seized his arm, but although he refused to mention it in Court, he confided to his brother, Sam, later, that she had seized his clothing in falling and this accounted for the disarray of his clothes on arrival at the station.

And so they travelled, he supporting her as she stood on the step outside the carriage, travelling at forty miles an hour between Woking and Esher. In evidence, Miss Dickinson said afterwards, he begged her to re-enter the carriage, saying that he would leave by the other door, anything if she would only return. She also said that but for him, she would have fallen. He had certainly saved her life, but she continued to scream.

A platelayer on the line saw with astonishment the extraordinary spectacle of a young lady screaming and standing on the high step of the carriage, hatless and supported only by the strong arm of a tall and distraught passenger in the train. He signalled to the driver, and the driver, looking back, saw her plight and notified the guard. By now there were a number of passengers leaning from their windows and imploring her to 'hold on tight'. Slowly and gradually the train drew grindingly to a halt at the next station, Esher, where the guard hurried back along the platform.

Miss Dickinson was lifted carefully to the ground by the guard. The tall passenger was heard to murmur, as she alighted 'Don't say anything – you will ruin me.' But from that moment Miss Rebecca Dickinson was determined to do just that.

Her hat was later recovered by the platelayer, who quite realised the importance of its loss and returned it to her. But nothing mollified her.

Now, at last, there were witnesses to the incident, but it was not surprising that sympathy was entirely with the young lady. Saying, with remarkable composure, that she was quite able to continue her journey, she was put into a carriage with another passenger, the Reverend Aubrey Browne. Valentine was locked into the next carriage with the two young men who had spoken to Miss Dickinson at the window. As the train started with a lurch once again, he remarked in some confusion how difficult it was to travel alone with a young lady – to which one of them replied: 'No wonder, with the state of your dress', and he saw that after the young lady had clutched at his waistband, to save herself from falling from the train, his clothes were now in disarray. He hastened to put it right and the rest of the journey travelled in an embarrassing silence, the young men silent and Valentine shocked and horrified at the turn that events had taken. He was shocked beyond measure to think of the results of a moment's indiscretion.

Miss Dickinson meanwhile was determined to justify her actions to her elder brother and also to the Reverend Aubrey Browne. On arrival at Waterloo both she and Valentine were led to the Station Master's office, where they gave their names and addresses. Mr Browne, having ordered a cab, escorted Miss Dickinson to her brother's house in Chesterfield Street.

The incident meant the loss of her holiday, but she was determined, and soon her brother was determined too that it should not mean the loss of her reputation. Valentine, meanwhile, was permitted to return home to his quarters in Aldershot.

That night, Sam and Florence, now Sir Samuel and Lady Baker, were having a dinner party at their lovely family home, Sandford Orleigh, in Devon, entertaining friends in their usual lavish style.

Sam was about to take the 'first lady' into the dining room, when the front door bell rang. This was most unusual at that hour, for punctuality was one of the rules of the household. Indeed, it was said that if the lady Sir Samuel was to take in to dinner was even a moment late, he would offer his arm to 'No. 2' – and when the confused and embarrassed first lady finally rustled into the dining room she would be greeted with cold disapproval.

So a ring at the bell at this critical moment was most unusual. A telegram was brought in. Sam tore it open, and, at once, realised that a very serious situation had developed. It was from his brother, Valentine, asking him to come at once.

With a polite bow to the company Sam at once ordered the carriage and his portmanteau to be packed. He wrote afterwards 'The house was full of people' – but with a farewell kiss to his lovely young wife, he stepped out into the darkness. The carriage was waiting. The horses clattered out of the drive and galloped towards Sandhurst.

10

THE TRIAL

On the very next day, 17 May, Valentine was asked to attend the Police Station at Guildford. The brothers had scarcely slept the night before, and Valentine had told Sam the whole astonishing story.

They drove to Guildford together, while Miss Dickinson travelled down with her barrister brother from London. There was no doubt that she had recovered her poise remarkably quickly, but her brother was determined not to let the matter rest.

Colonel Valentine Baker still could not believe that he would be charged with a very serious offence, although naturally desperately anxious for his reputation. He offered to speak to Miss Dickinson's brother, and settle the matter between them privately, but it was of no avail. The case was postponed until 24 June so that he could prepare his defence.

Sam put up surety of £1,000 and Valentine's great friend, Lord Valentia, shocked beyond measure that his Colonel should have been accused, later also put up £1,000. Lord Valentia had so often ridden beside Valentine, and had twice won the Regimental Steeplechase in 1869 and 1871, in both years winning 'Baker's Cup'. It seemed quite unbelievable that his beloved Colonel could be accused of any sort of misconduct.

On 25 June Sam was to write to Lord Wharncliffe:

> With regard to Val's affair, I know more from him than I have a right to divulge. He has confided *the whole* to three friends, including myself, but you know in such a case a man is at the mercy of a lady, and his tongue must on a point of honour be absolutely sealed . . . in a court of law. This places him at a ruinous disadvantage when it comes to *Law*.

At the same time Val must allow that his best friends cannot defend even as much as he confesses. Then, on the other hand, men are not all Josephs, and we must all admit that it was lucky for Joseph that he did not meet Mrs. Potiphar alone in a railway compartment . . .

I trust the Dickinson family will not press the matter further, as to me it appears disastrous to all concerned.

Sam could write to his friend fairly cheerfully, knowing that his brother was quite innocent of any evil intent towards Miss Dickenson and that a lighthearted kiss was all that he had intended or, perhaps, some words, meant as a compliment, had been taken by her in the wrong way. However, the storm clouds were gathering.

Valentine was refused a special jury of his peers. For already the case had drawn public attention, and was rapidly becoming almost a 'cause célèbre'. A scurrilous pamphlet had been produced in London, and in Surrey, according to the Magistrate, Colonel Marshall, before whom Valentine had appeared: 'At the present time a very strong feeling exists against him in the county, more especially among the classes of society from which common juries are selected.'

He continued, 'I am convinced that under these circumstances, he is more likely to get a fair and impartial trial before a special jury than before a common jury at the Assizes. These reports are malicious and totally without foundation.'

But the rumours spread like wildfire. Miss Dickinson was looked upon as a heroine, willing to save her honour even by risking death, while Valentine was considered a 'monster'. The trial was not postponed, but arranged for the Assizes at Croydon on 2 August, a Bank Holiday, in the Crown Court.

It was also very unfortunate that the incident should take place just when public opinion was running very highly against those who had purchased their Commissions. Cardwell's reforms had concentrated on the abolition of the system, only five years earlier, and at this time the popularity of the Army was at a very low ebb. It had been twenty years since the Crimean War, and public memory is often short and forgets the achievements of its heroes.

Even in America, Mark Twain wrote a particularly venomous article about the case and claimed that it was typical of the sort of thing that went on in British high circles.

The intervening months must have been agonising for Valentine, but at last the day of the trial drew near, and we have a letter from Valentine's sister showing the devotion and loyalty of his friends and family.

11. **HRH The Prince of Wales, Colonel-in-Chief, The Tenth Hussars accompanied by Colonel Valentine Baker at the Royal Review in Aldershot, 1870** *(From a photograph presented to Mrs Anne Baker by the Tenth Royal Hussars)*

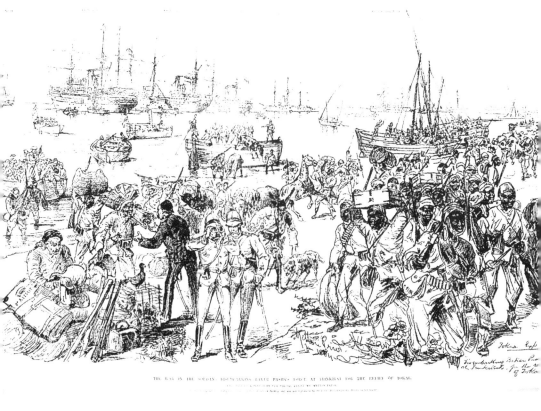

THE WAR IN THE SOUDAN: DISEMBARKING BAKER PASHA'S FORCE AT TRINKITAT FOR THE RELIEF OF TOKAR.

12. **Disembarking Baker Pasha's force at Trinkitat for the relief of Tokar.**

13. **Baker Pasha inspecting the forts at Massowar** *(Both sketches are by Welton Prior for the Illustrated London News, 1884)*

14. Major General Charles Gordon

15. Earl Kitchener of Khartoum

(Sir Hubert von Herkomer, 1890 – National Portrait Gallery)

16. Sybil (aged 14)

17. Hermione

Valentine and Fanny's beloved daughters

18. 4 February 1884. The defeat of Baker Pasha's force at El Teb in its attempt to relieve Tokar. Valentine Baker (left centre) on his famous white horse, accompanied by Colonel Burnaby. Major Harvey is in the foreground.

4 *Duke Street,*
St James.
August 2nd 1875

Dearest Rob,

I came up this morning and am staying here until the train starts for St Pancras. The scenes I have been through are terrible. I cannot attempt to tell you till we meet. I would not have missed my farewell parting with Val last night for the world. He had to leave the Hut ['The Hut' was the name describing his quarters at Aldershot] at *3 am.* There was no other train in the morning that was safe to trust to – so he will have got no rest.

I grieve that you were not able to stay for the trial to-day. We wanted him to be well supported. I think he will be. Sir Richard Airey, Sir Thomas Steele, Colonel Oakes, Colonel Shute and a number of others have gone. Fanny and Mrs and Miss Wormald bore up wonderfully. Fanny has gone to Croydon to-day, to catch five minutes with Val, after all was over. This was entirely against my advice, for fear of a scene, and I know Val would hate a scene.

There was no 'scene', but this letter does show how faithfully his family and friends stood by him. The Marquis of Tavistock, Lord Lucan, Viscount Halifax and many other distinguished men who Valentine counted as his friends, were also in court.

But Sam had been right. As an officer and a gentleman, Valentine would not dispute the word of a lady, and he positively refused to allow his Counsel to cross examine Miss Dickinson. Agonising although it must have been for him, he would say nothing in his own defence.

* * *

2 August, 1875, was an immensely hot and stifling day and, as it was a Bank Holiday, the streets outside the Court were crowded. The trial was to be before Mr Justice Brett, well-known for his severity – and from the account in *The Times* on the following day one can see that it had attracted a great deal of attention.

From as early as 8 o'clock in the morning, the account runs, people had begun to assemble round the doors of the Court, and long before the time for opening them a dense crowd had congregated before the court-house, and not only obstructed the entrance, but completely blocked up the roadway before and for some distance on each side of the court-house. No case has ever been within living memory which appears to have caused such excitement. It is hardly necessary to say that the court was densely crowded in every part. . . . It was with the utmost difficulty that the counsel in the case, as they arrived, could force their way to their places, and the court was from time to time disturbed by the cries of the vast crowd outside. Colonel Baker, with his attorney, appeared long before the time appointed . . . and was soon followed by his Counsel, Mr Hawkins QC and Mr Sergeant Ballantine. Mr Sergeant Parry and Mr Poland appeared on the part of the prosecution. It was clear that distinguished counsel had been engaged on both sides. At half past ten the learned Judge took his seat on the Bench. Colonel Valentine Baker was at once called, and pleaded 'Not Guilty' in a firm voice.

Although outwardly calm, Valentine Baker must have felt he was living through a nightmare.

Before him were the judge and jury in that crowded court, and also near him he recognised some of his greatest friends, and those he most admired, who had come especially to support him. Lord Lucan, was there – the gallant old General who had commanded the cavalry in the Crimean War – and who would have spoken for him if he could, his elder brother Sam, who had stood by him all through the last few weeks, Sir Richard Airey, who had once appointed Nolan as his Aide-de-Camp and who was now Adjutant General to the Army, and Sir Thomas Steele, who was in command at Aldershot, with other very close friends. All his pride as a soldier came to his aid, and he stood motionless while the trial for something of which he felt he was innocent proceeded.

The jury was sworn in, but there was such a commotion in the street outside that it was some time before Sergeant Parry could rise.

He described the three fold charge which must have seemed quite horrifying to Valentine. He was charged with attempted rape, indecent assault and common assault. At this point the Judge had to order the street outside to be cleared so great was the noise.

The train journey on that fatal day in May was then described by the Sergeant. It was stated that nothing untoward had occurred until the train reached Woking Station. It was soon after leaving the station that the young lady had described her travelling companion as changing completely, seizing her hand, kissing her passionately and forcing her in terror to fling herself out of the carriage on to the step, where she stood in the utmost 'peril and alarm'.

Miss Dickinson was then herself called – and she came in 'supported by her mother and a sister' – she gave her evidence as coolly and calmly as on the previous occasion. She described the journey and how she had chatted happily until the train reached Woking. How the defendant had then seated himself beside her, and had taken her hand and asked if he might kiss her. She described how she sprang up to press the emergency bell, how the bell did not work, and how she first leant out of the window and screamed – and how she continued screaming so loudly that others in the train heard her, and how she eventually stepped out backwards on to the running board of the train. She said that Colonel Baker had begged her to re-enter the carriage saying he would leave by the other door, but although she mentioned those things, it seemed that the judge and jury were quite unable to put any favourable interpretation upon his actions. They seemed unable to realise that as soon as she began to scream or even to seem upset, the Colonel would certainly have been really alarmed for his own reputation, and when she actually spoke to the two young men in the adjoining carriage he would have been acutely aware of his own embarrassing position. Although she described him as seizing her, in reality he might only have been attempting to restrain her from pressing the bell, or falling out of the train. There were no witnesses, and it was his word as an officer and a gentleman against hers.

He would not allow his counsel Mr Hawkins to cross-examine her. 'I was debarred' Hawkins wrote long afterwards 'from putting a single question.'

Sam's words proved only too true, 'In such a case a man is at the mercy of a lady, and his tongue must on a point of honour be sealed. . .'

All through her evidence, Valentine stood with his face white and set in the dock, and Miss Rebecca Dickinson showed him no pity.

The bricklayer who first saw her outside the carriage then gave evidence, and the platelayer, followed by the guard, who had lifted Miss Dickinson from the train.

The fact that the Colonel's clothing was ruffled and in disarray on his arrival at the Station was noticed by the guard and the two young men in the railway carriage, but Miss Dickinson had never mentioned it, and had only said that he had 'insulted her'. Meanwhile the Colonel's code of honour prevented him from involving a lady in any accusation whatever.

When the Reverend Aubrey Browne was called upon to give evidence, he merely said that Miss Dickinson was very much distressed, and had evidently suffered great alarm, though at the same time she had great self-control.

Colonel Baker's full statement to the Magistrates was then read: he said:

87

I am placed here in the most delicate and difficult position. If any act of mine could have given any annoyance to Miss Dickinson I beg to express to her my unqualified regret. At the same time I solemnly declare upon my honour that the case was not as it has been represented by her to-day under the influence of exaggerated fear and unnecessary alarm. To the evidence of the police constable I give the most unqualified denial. I don't in the least intend to say that she wilfully misrepresented the case, but that she has represented it incorrectly, no doubt under the influence of exaggerated fear and unnecessary alarm.

The judge's final summing-up contained these words, which in our more charitable age may seem strange: 'If a man kisses a woman against her will, and with criminal passion and intent, such an act is indecent assault. A kiss that gratifies or incites passion is indecent.'

Working up to a climax, the judge continued, 'The mere laying of a man's hand on a woman amounts to criminal assault.'

The jury, following the judge's advice, took only a quarter of an hour to decide on the verdict. Colonel Valentine was pronounced innocent of the first, most serious charge, but he was found 'guilty' on the two other counts.

It was then, and only then, that Sir Richard Airey was able to speak in defence of his brother officer. He said that he had watched Valentine Baker's career with the greatest interest, and knew him 'to have attained a brilliant reputation as a cavalry officer'. Sir Richard was Adjutant General to the Army and he said it was his business to know the character of his officers and he had never known anything to Colonel Baker's discredit.

Sir Thomas Steele, in command at Aldershot, also gave strong evidence in favour of Colonel Baker, both as an officer and a man of honour. But the jury had already given their verdict – it could not be altered. And the judge, in spite of this evidence was to impose a very harsh sentence – Colonel Valentine Baker was to serve twelve months in the common prison, he was to pay a fine of £500, a great deal in those days, and pay the costs of the prosecution.

The Court eventually rose, Miss Dickinson, without a glance at the Colonel, left the court with her brother and the crowd gradually melted away.

The terrible case was over. Night fell, the crowd, which had dispersed so slowly, was soon to forget the drama of that long hot Bank Holiday Monday. But for Valentine Baker all was not over.

All that he had worked for, all he had hoped to achieve in his life and everything he had lived for, seemed lost to him, and his self-assurance and confidence seemed to be torn away from him, as the iron doors of Horseferry jail closed behind him. But his courage, so much a part of the Baker character, never once deserted him, perhaps because he was convinced of his own innocence, and the fact that he had acted in court as an officer and a gentleman.

His counsel, Mr Hawkins, well known to be a hard man, and one who was later to become known as a 'Hanging Judge', could not help saying afterwards: 'I say to his honour, that as a Gentleman and a British Officer, he preferred to take to himself the ruin of his own character, the forfeiture of his own commission in the Army, the loss of his social status, and all that would make life worth having, to cast even a doubt on the lady's veracity in the witness-box.' Mr Hawkins added: 'The manliness of his defence showed him naturally to be a man of honour, who, having been guilty of severe misconduct, did all he could to amend the wrong he had done, and so he won my sympathy in his sad misfortune and misery.' It was said later that the nobility in Valentine Baker's character had appealed to the nobility in that of his Counsel, for Mr Hawkins had the courage to speak out for a man who everyone at that time condemned.

11

VICTORIAN INDICTMENT

The day after that fatal Bank Holiday dawned bright and sunny at the Queen's favourite holiday home, Osborne, on the Isle of Wight. Queen Victoria had arrived only two days earlier, but she had been very upset by an event which had occurred on her journey. Travelling by the Royal Train with Princess Beatrice, she had journeyed delightfully along the special Royal line by Alverstoke, Vectis Road and Stokes Bay, but once at sea, the Royal Yacht, the 'Albert' had unfortunately been in collision with a small private boat, the 'Mistletoe', very soon after putting to sea in the Solent. The Queen herself was seated on deck at the time and did all she could to help the survivors, being restrained by Lord Ponsonby from helping even more. Two of the crew of the 'Mistletoe' were unfortunately drowned and Queen Victoria was devestated.

However, on 3 August, three days later, she was hoping to enjoy a peaceful and happy holiday. However, on opening the papers on the terrace after breakfast, yet another shock was to meet her eyes.

She was to write in her Diary that evening:

> Read the Article in The Times, the Daily News and the Daily Telegraph of that dreadful disgraceful outrage on Miss Dickinson for which Colonel V. Baker is being tried.
>
> Spoke to Arthur [the Duke of Connaught] about it, and he said it was a dreadful business, that Colonel Baker was at that time Quarter Master General at Aldershot, and had been preparing for the Manoeuvres. Colonel Baker, who formerly was Colonel of Bertie's Regiment, is brother to the traveller, Sir Samuel Baker.

It was heartbreaking that the Queen should have read the account in the newspapers, coloured, as it was bound to be, by the sensation which the trial had caused, before hearing an account of the incident from her eldest son. There was so much of which she could not approve. First, there were the Baker brothers themselves, friends of the Prince of Wales. She also knew that Valentine was a member of the dashing Marlborough Club. Sir Samuel Baker, it is true, had been knighted by her in the White Drawing Room at Buckingham Palace in 1866 on his return from his great discovery of the Lake Albert Nyanza, but she had not 'received' his beautiful young Hungarian wife, whom he had met on his travels, even though the Prince of Wales had recommended her most warmly to his mother.

Eight years later the Queen was still worried about her son's many unconventional friends, and did not realise that he had a talent for recognising true loyalty and enterprise, and that originality and vigour were refreshing to him.

Now she was horrified that Sir Samuel's younger brother, Valentine, who until recently had been Colonel of the 10th Hussars, should have become involved in such a totally wild and impossible scandal. She felt every sympathy with Miss Dickinson. Not only was the Queen deeply disapproving of the scandal, but she felt her beloved railways were in danger of losing their reputation for safety and reliability if subjected to such scandals. For Queen Victoria was the first Monarch to use the railway regularly.

Queen Victoria's saloon, on the London North Western Railway, started life as two six-wheeled vehicles, connected by a flexible gangway – the very first to be fitted in the country. The saloon was beautifully furnished in mahogany and silk, and joined private bedrooms for herself and Princess Beatrice and a comfortable sitting-room and small kitchen. She could travel to Scotland frequently in comfort, where on arrival, a red carpet would be rolled out for her at the small Scottish station near Ballater.

So it seemed to her, that Miss Dickinson had been terribly wronged, and that Colonel Baker was, indeed, all that the crowd outside the court-room thought of him, and that nothing short of his disgrace could be considered.

As soon as the case was lost, Valentine had offered his resignation to the Horse Guards, but after such a verdict, it seemed possible that he might be cashiered. The final decision, however, rested with the Queen herself.

The Duke of Cambridge, Commander-in-Chief of the Army, and the Prince of Wales could hardly believe that such a disaster could have befallen one whom they esteemed so highly, and the Duke, according to

Lord Ponsonby, wrote immediately after the trial, asking the Queen if she would accept Colonel Baker's resignation and not dismiss him from the Service. Lord Ponsonby wrote: 'The Duke wrote that a man ought not to be punished twice for the same offence.' Lord Ponsonby himself suggested that he should not lose the value of his Commission, but the Queen would not be persuaded.

During July, letters passed frequently between the Duke of Cambridge and the Queen, for the Duke realised that the Army was in danger of losing one of its most brilliant leaders. But it was all to no avail.

On 30 August, Sir Henry Ponsonby was to write to the Duke once more:

> The Queen desires me to assure your Royal Highness that she never for a moment thought that your Royal Highness defended the conduct of the prisoner, but that she desired to explain to your Royal Highness how necessary her Majesty thought it, that this man should be removed from the Army with a mark of disgrace, and not be permitted to retire.
> I have the honour to be, Sir,
>> Your Royal Highness's
>> Obedient and Humble Servant,
>> Henry F. Ponsonby.

A notice appeared soon afterwards in the London Gazette:

> Lieutenant Colonel, Brevet Colonel Valentine Baker, half pay, late 10th Hussars, has been removed from the Army, Her Majesty having no further use for his services.

It was a decision which was to alter the course of Valentine's life; but also, perhaps, the course of history. For in the next few vital years, England was to be deprived of one of her most brilliant soldiers, Turkey was to gain a great General who was to save her an army and, much later, Egypt was to gain a devoted Administrator and friend.

Two letters from Sam to Lord Wharncliffe, written in July, 1875, are still preserved. In the first, he wrote:

> . . . we would be very happy were it not for this sad affair of Val's. Although he has been guilty of much indiscretion the punishment is terribly severe in proportion to the offence. In such cases a gentleman's tongue is sealed, but no man of common sense can suppose that he acted without some attraction that he accepted as an encouragement . . .

In the second letter he wrote:

> My own opinion would suggest that Miss Dickinson has now a fine oppor-
> tunity to become a heroine – Val spared her a cross-examination, he should
> therefore be entitled to some sympathy. In about six weeks the young lady
> should *herself* petition the Queen on Val's behalf. If she were to take this
> generous line of conduct she would take a much higher position than by tri-
> umphing over Val as a ruined victim.

But this hopeful thought by his kind brother was not to occur to the
family of Miss Ruth Rebecca Dickinson.

It was a shattering blow to Valentine Baker, but as Disraeli was to
describe him later, he was 'no ordinary man'. From the very first, he
was determined to fight back for the reputation he had lost. Friends and
comrades soon crowded to see him. It was said that his wife's loyal little
cousin, Fanny Wormald, who was forbidden by her father to visit him,
defied her papa's instructions, and came to see him in prison. She
remained an unfailing friend to both the Bakers through the next difficult years. It was even said in the family that the Prince of Wales
himself visited him, and rumours began to spread of parties and
laughter coming from Horseferry Jail. These rumours were hotly denied
in the pages of *Vanity Fair*, whose editor always upheld Valentine's
innocence, and commented on the harshness of the sentence.

His friends kept him in good heart, although Fanny was to write to
The Times after the first three months were over, the time of the most
deep depression for her husband:

> I am thankful to state that the symptoms which recently caused so much
> alarm, both to myself and his friends and family have yielded to medical
> treatment.
>   I cannot, however, hide from myself the terrible fact that such continued
> and trying confinement after his active and useful life, has rendered him
> finally out of health, and his condition causes me the most constant and dis-
> tressing anxiety.

But the authorities were unyielding, and the months dragged by.

★   ★   ★

As a direct result of the case, triangular windows were first of all introduced into all trains between carriages, and very soon corridor trains
were established, entirely as a result of the case. In 1879, the first 'Res-

taurant Car' made travelling a more comfortable as well as a more social affair. In addition, 'Ladies Only' carriages were introduced, only being finally discontinued in 1975, a hundred years later, when the case of Valentine Baker was mentioned as the cause of their introduction. Altogether it was realised that no man's honour could be safe, if he travelled alone in a railway carriage with a lady of doubtful virtue, or, in fact, as in Valentine Baker's case, even with a lady of the most stainless character.

For many years, military fathers warned their sons not to travel alone with a lady in a closed carriage – because of the disaster which had befallen one of their distinguished fellow-officers . . . and more sophisticated London business men advised each other to light a large cigar when in the presence of a lady alone in a railway compartment, so that the ash could be shown not to have been disturbed in the event of an aspersion on their honour.

Altogether, wild rumours circulated and the Army realised it had lost one of its most promising leaders, on grounds which, to those who knew Valentine well, were completely out of character. One of the very few friends in whom Valentine had confided was his brother Sam. Years later, when Sir Reginald Wingate became Sir Samuel's close friend and met his brother Valentine, he was told the true story of the happenings in the railway carriage so long ago. When writing his father's biography, Sir Ronald Wingate referred to this:

> He met among others, General Valentine Baker. Baker was the brother of Sir Samuel Baker. . . . He had commanded the 10th Hussars, but had had to resign his commission owing to a scandal in which he was, in fact, the innocent party.

TURKEY: ON SPECIAL SERVICE

12

EXILE

In the summer of 1876, just a year after the trial, Valentine was released and, owing to the kind intervention of the Prince of Wales, he was offered the appointment of head of the Turkish Gendarmerie at Constantinople, with the rank of Major General.

But though he was to serve brilliantly abroad, he was never to serve in the British Army again. With true friendship the Prince of Wales was not to forget him, and he, the Duke of Cambridge and Sir Garnet Wolseley, were tireless in their efforts to persuade the Queen to restore him to his commission. But the Queen felt unable to change her mind, until it was too late.

Although the appointment in Turkey meant a separation from his wife and beloved small daughters, to whom he was devoted, for Valentine and virtual exile from his own country, the Prince of Wales had shown an intuitive insight into his character in arranging an appointment for him. It was an opportunity which he could develop in the future, with his special knowledge of the Eastern Question and his genius for organisation. It seemed that the ordeal through which he had passed, and which might have broken a lesser spirit, was only to increase his determination to win back his reputation, and to justify the faith the Prince of Wales had placed in him.

The *Clouds in the East* which he had foreseen had already gathered darkly on the horizon, but it was not even the Russian menace to Turkey and Persia which was to trigger hostilities.

In mid-summer, 1875, after a series of bad harvests, the warlike Serbs of Herzegovina had risen against the heavy taxes imposed by the Turks, and soon the rising, helped by volunteers from Serbia, was to engulf Bosnia.

Count Andrassy had done his best to arrange reforms and a peaceful settlement, but by the summer of 1876 the armies of Serbia and Montenegro had joined the rebellion, encouraged by the Russians.

Most disastrously, on 8 May, a party of 'Bashi Bazouks', free-booting Turkish irregulars, had raided the small Bulgarian town of Batok, and had murdered five thousand inhabitants, men, women and children. It was a terrible crime, reported a month later in the English newspapers.

At once Gladstone, from his retirement home in Hawarden, denounced the Turks in a fiercely indignant pamphlet. His support of the Christian Serbs extended to Christian Russia. He denounced Turkey and with his usual rhetoric he ended his pamphlet calling on 'Their Zapheks and their Mudirs, their Bimbashis and their Yuzbashis, their Kaimakams and their Pashas, one and all, bag and baggage, shall I hope, clear out from the Province they have desolated and profaned.' Such rhetoric, however well deserved, was bound to embarrass the British Government, and especially the Prime Minister, Benjamin Disraeli, to whom the threat of Russian expansion seemed ever-present. Valentine was to find himself thrown at once into the centre of the struggle – with his knowledge of Russian expansion he was, perhaps, the most useful observer of the situation which the Government could have in his new appointment. For at that time, there was no official Intelligence Service. In the Foreign Office and Diplomacy, the Prime Minister had only two sources of information available to him on Foreign Affairs – newspaper correspondents and private individuals whom they could trust. It was therefore not surprising that when Valentine had been only a few months in Constantinople he returned briefly, and reported to the Duke of Cambridge and the Prince of Wales. Francis Knollys was to write from Marlborough House on 10 December:

> My dear Monty,
>   The Prince of Wales desires me to ask you whether Lord Beaconsfield would like to see Colonel Baker before he returns to Turkey.
>   The Duke of Cambridge and HRH have both seen him privately, and, I need hardly say, they have found him most interesting.
>   Yours, Francis Knollys.

This meeting was followed by a long letter from Valentine, out in Turkey once more, written to the Prince of Wales, on 6 November:

In Camp, Near DERKOS
Nov. 6th 1876

Dear Sir,

You kindly told me that I might write to you, and I will not allow any longer time to elapse without sending you information that may be interesting relative to the present serious crisis in Turkey.

The acceptance of the ultimatum of Russia, imposing an unconditional six weeks' armistice has staved off the outbreak of a Turkey/Russia War for a time.

But I am convinced only for a time. Public feeling in Russia, already much aroused, will be more than excited by recent Turkish successes, and by the heavy rule of Russian officers, and it will prove too strong for the humane wishes of the Emperor.

But a war between Turkey and Russia menaces English interests so closely, that we are sure to be, in some way, involved.

The united action of the Powers in favour of a Peace must be futile, for their interests are different, and real united action is impossible. England could not suffer Constantinople to fall into the hands of Russia, but it inevitably would do so without an English occupation. The Turks have concentrated their whole available Army against Serbia and Montenegro, and have denuded other important strategical positions of troops. In cases of a sudden outbreak of war the road to Constantinople lies open. Russia by means of the Roumanian railway could concentrate 50,000 men at . . . . .* on the Danube in a few days. She might then cross near Kutchuk, and marching to Shumla, seize the Balkan passes and occupy the important positions of Karnabat. From there she could push on, unopposed, to Constantinople. For the Russians at Kutchuk would, by map distances, be 100 miles from Karnabat, and 255 miles to Constantinople, whereas the Turkish army at . . . . .* is 250 miles from Karnabat and 460 to Constantinople.

The question thus arises whether England, without allies, can prevent a Russian occupation of the Bosphorus.

It is very natural that we should doubt, as Austria, by her hesitations, has invariably antagonised every power that has trusted in her.

Since my arrival at Constantinople I have been minutely studying the probable strategical situation, and I am convinced that if England will act boldly and independently she wants no allies but can hold her own against any European combination.

It is only necessary for us to secure absolutely the Bosphorus and the Dardanelles against a Russian occupation. I have been devoting myself to this object and I have found a most admirable military position about twenty-five miles from Constantinople, which stretches from the Black Sea to the Sea of Marmora. This might be so strengthened in a short time by fieldworks, that a force of 100,000 men could protect Constantinople against any numbers that could be brought against it. No difficulty arises in protecting the narrow approach to the Dardanelles. If Russia invades Turkey, England should be prepared to immediately occupy this position.

Any difficulty in producing so large a force as 100,000 might be met by taking Turkish troops into British pay and giving them a proportion of British officers. There are no finer soldiers in the world than the men of the present Turkish Army, and English service might be so popular that we might raise any number of them. The fortifications of these lines and the secure command of the Straits and the Black Sea which they would give to our Navy, would make English interests perfectly secure, and we could then calmly await events, without the necessity of any allies, who must only fail and hamper our activities.

In case of Russia declaring war on us, we might simply hold this position, and blockade all her ports until she gave in. We might assume that a Russian occupation of Bulgaria would not remain long unopposed by some other Powers, more especially as it would involve her command of the Danube.

I know, Sir, that you would like to hear of my personal movements. So much jealousy has existed relative to the employment of foreign officers and the political position has been so complicated, that I have not entered the Turkish service. But in case of war with Russia, I believe that I should have an opportunity of doing so at once, and in a high position.

All my time has been spent in reconnoitring the positions to which I have alluded. Before leaving England I had suggested the importance of this line to the military authorities, and an Engineer Officer has been sent out to survey it. His view invariably coincides with mine. We have had very bad weather for camping out, but our survey will be completed in a few days. I then intend to return to England for a short time, coming back here at the expiration of the armistice.

With many thanks to you, dear Sir, for all the kind interest you have ever taken in all that might benefit me,

Believe me, Sir,

Dutifully yours,
V. Baker. *

The last paragraph of the letter shows how deeply grateful Valentine Baker was to His Royal Highness.

Meanwhile newspaper correspondents were gathering in Constantinople in anticipation of war. George Augustus Sale, representing the *Daily*

---

* This letter is reproduced from the Royal Archives at Windsor by Gracious Permission of Her Majesty, Queen Elizabeth II. Two place names have been omitted as illegible.

Telegraph, Gallega of *The Times* and even the redoubtable Colonel Burnaby passed through on his way to Kars and Batum on a fact-finding expedition which he was to publish later, *On Horse-Back Through Asia Minor* – a fitting sequel to his *Ride to Khiva* published only a year earlier.

Burnaby was setting forth on a two thousand mile ride, something on which Valentine Baker would have loved to accompany him, and after which he implored the Turks to strengthen their defences.

On 24 April, while Burnaby's book was still being written, Russia declared war on Turkey and immediately started to invade Kars. Batum alone resisted and the Russians advanced southward towards Ezerum.

As soon as war broke out, the Turkish Grand Vizier proposed that General Valentine Baker should act as Military Adviser to the Commander-in-Chief on the European front and the aged Abdul Kerim, at Shumla – but the War Minister, Redif Pasha, did not approve of foreign officers in the Turkish Army, and cancelled the order.

Valentine contracted a bad attack of typhoid and for three months he could take no part in active operations.

On his recovery, he must however have been informed that should the Russians advance across the border, he would be given an opportunity to serve in some capacity in the Turkish Army for, in a letter dated 31 May, Sir Francis Knollys was writing on behalf of the Prince of Wales to Valentine's eldest brother, Sam:–

> *Marlborough House,*
> *Pall Mall S.W.*
> *May 31st 1877*

My dear Sir Samuel,
    I have shown your brother's note to the Prince of Wales who desires me to express the pleasure which he experiences at hearing that he has recovered from his late illness and is employed in a position which is agreeable to him in the Turkish Army.
    Pray say all this to your brother in his Royal Highness's name when you next write to him.

Believe me, yours sincerely,
Francis Knollys.

But it is doubtful if this kind message reached Valentine for many months, for only a few days after it was written, in June, the Russian Army under General Guorko crossed the Danube in strength, and without serious resistance, was able to reach the Balkan Mountains. The only real resistance came from Osman Pasha, who managed to outwit them, and moved his forces into Plevna, thus threatening the Russian flank in their march southward to Adrianople.

The danger was only too evident, Redif was hastily dismissed, and Abdul Kerim was replaced at Shumla by Mehemit Ali, a brilliant commander, who although originally a German, had been brought up in Constantinople.

'Baker Pasha' as he was then known, was immediately called in as Military Adviser to Mehemit Ali, with the rank of Lieutenant General. It was exactly the moment when all Valentine's training as a military commander could come into play. He immediately, although tactfully, helped Mehemit Ali to dispose of his available forces in such a way that the Russians were forced to halt in their advance. In his book *War in Bulgaria* he modestly describes how he reported the disposition of the Russian forces, and how he realised that the Turks were up against the whole Russian B Corps. On receiving this report, the Turks invited Valentine to remain as a 'General available for Special Services', which meant that he could literally take part in the actual fighting. As the Turkish forces were numerically so low in numbers compared to those of the enemy, Valentine arranged that the advance companies should fire from concealed positions in brushwood, so that their lack of numbers would not be known. Under the weight of this concealed fire, the Russian line wavered and fell back in confusion. He said, 'It was one of those extraordinary chances of war when a great risk must be run for a great result'. Valentine then rode forward on his grey horse, accompanied by his staff, giving the Russians the impression that he was backed up by reinforcements. For two hours he and his gallant band held the position until relieved.

Valentine was determined to follow up this success with an advance, and after a conference with the Marshal, Prince Hassan al Sali, Pasha, it was decided to go forward, covered by gunfire. He wrote, 'I felt it was time that I once again took an active part.'

The ensuing action was described very vividly by a war correspondent (as reported in the Regimental History of the 10th Hussars) then attached to the Turkish forces, who watched the ensuing battle with amazement. He wrote:

> Eight squadrons of Turkish Regular Cavalry came out from behind a low hill on the Turkish right. They were led by a man on a fine grey Arab, the finest horseman I have ever seen. They came round the hill at a trot, then broke into a gallop and came swooping down on the left flank of the

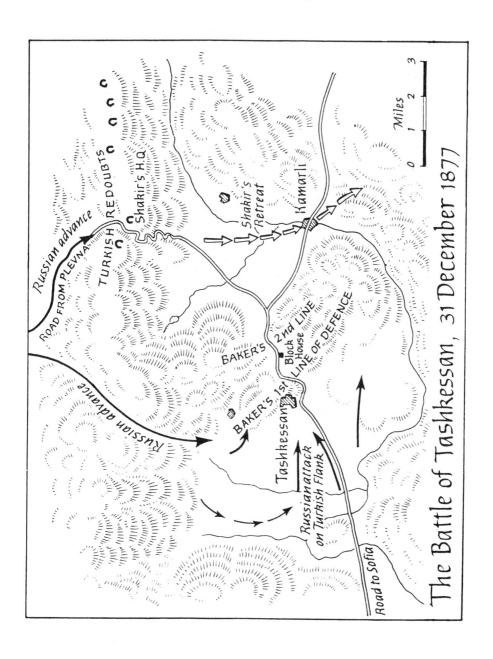

The Battle of Tashkessan, 31 December 1877

Russian advance

ROAD FROM PLEVNA

TURKISH REDOUBTS

Shakir's H.Q.

Shakir's Retreat

Kamarli

Russian advance

BAKER'S

2nd LINE

Block House

LINE OF DEFENCE

BAKER'S 1st

Tashkessan

Russian attack on Turkish Flank

Road to Sofia

Miles

0 1 2 3

Russians, tearing through them like an express train through a flock of sheep. I could not help watching the man on the grey Arab, and I saw his sabre go sweeping up and down and all around like lightning flashes. He made a lane through the Russian ranks in whatever direction he went.

Some bodies of the Russian Cavalry came out to meet him and they came into contact in a large field of maize. But there was no holding back Baker and his Turks, and the Russian cavalry was soon tearing back as hard as they could go, to get under the shelter of their guns. The Turkish cavalry followed them hard like tigers who had once tasted blood and longed for more. I saw a shell explode within a few yards of Baker Pasha; his brave horse fell, and down he came. That was the end of the grey Arab, but not of his master, for Baker was up in a moment, on the charger of a common trooper, in the middle of his men, hacking like a very Hercules.

An old Turkish artillery officer who was standing quite close to me, laid down his field glasses, and said: 'I swear by the Prophet, that the Infidel who commands our cavalry fights with the courage of ten thousand tigers.' 'And yet,' said another young artillery officer, 'Allah has smitten the English with such blindness that they allow a man like him to leave their Army.

The Russian defeat became a rout, but Baker was disappointed that Kerim had not actually followed the enemy, and felt that an opportunity had been lost. On his return to the camp, he was presented with the decoration of the Osmanie by Sulieman Pasha, who said how glad he was that General Valentine Baker himself had been spared although his poor horse had been killed.

By November, 1877, the situation had so far improved that the Russians were driven back beyond the Balkan mountains, while Mehemit Ali was at Sofia, organising an army for the relief of Plevna. For the Russians had previously surrounded the town and their brilliant engineer Todleben was already throwing up fortifications.

In spite of this the *Daily Telegraph* Correspondent in the city, Dew Gay, escaped. His was a 'Story from the Inside' – and Fred Burnaby, reading it at home, could not bear to think that he was separated from the action. He at once took ship to Constantinople and made his way towards the scene of the war, officially, as 'the Travelling Agent of the Stafford House Committee' which had been set up by the Duke of Sutherland to provide medical services for the Turks.

It was pure chance that on one dull cloudy November morning, when Valentine stood on the draughty platform of the railway station at Adrianople, he should catch sight of the towering form and broad shoulders which could not possibly belong to any other than his great friend Fred Burnaby of the Blues.

With amazement the two friends greeted one another – Valentine was even less easy to recognise, in his Turkish Army greatcoat and fez, but, delighting in each other's company, they determined to continue their journey to Sofia together. Fred Burnaby explained the reason for his journey, and how he was determined to enter the city of Plevna itself. Valentine was horrified. Since Gay had escaped, the Russian lines had been drawn more closely round the city, and even if Burnaby evaded the armed patrols beyond the Balkans, he would not be able to pass the investing forces. Even if he succeeded, he would probably be shot by the defending Turks.

Valentine must also have told his friend of the depressing outlook for the defence of Turkey. Thousands of Russian soldiers were pouring over the frontier, and it was only a matter of time before they engulfed the passes over the mountains and the road to Sofia. For as long as he could, Valentine was determined to stem their advance, but the outlook was very grim. Plevna itself could not hold out much longer. Burnaby agreed to talk over his plan with Mehemit Ali and the two friends continued their journey together. At Sofia, however, they heard that Mehemit Ali had left for the Front and was already supervising the artillery fire at the Orkhranie Pass, through which runs the main Sofia/Plevna Road.

When they reached Mehemit Ali at his headquarters, they found him fearfully depressed. Valentine tried to dissuade him from exposing himself to the enemy fire, but he replied that the only way he could save his honour was by being killed or wounded himself. He told them that the Russians were threatening to outflank him by pushing through the mountains on his left – his own soldiers were deserting in thousands. He felt sure that when he sent back this news he would be disgraced and recalled.

In *War in Bulgaria*, Valentine quoted Mehemit Ali's advice to Burnaby – 'You are an English officer, full of energy and courage, but there are plans which are so hazardous that it becomes folly to attempt them . . . and I feel so strongly that you would be throwing away your life for no useful purpose that I must urgently advise you to give up all thought of proceeding further with your enterprise.' Burnaby at last agreed and when the news came through no less than a week later that Plevna had surrendered he could not but acknowledge the wisdom of Mehemit Ali's advice.

One afternoon, when Valentine went to pay his usual respects to Mehemit Ali, he found the tent empty. As the Commander-in-Chief had anticipated, his despatch to Constantinople had led to his recall. Shakir Pasha was now left alone to defend the Orkhranie Pass.

★ ★ ★

For a few days, intense cold and mist hung over the battlefield, preventing any serious engagements, but the forward troops of the Russian Army were well within sight of the Turkish Headquarters. A war correspondent with the Russians, Archibald Forbes, approached Count Schouvaloff, the local commander, and asked if any English officers were recognisable on the Turkish side. Schouvaloff replied:

> 'Yes, indeed, quite a number! You can see them for yourself if you go up yonder. Two of them are old friends of mine, and I ask for nothing better than to invite them to come over and dine with me. You are too young to have been in the Aldershot autumn manoeuvres of 1871, else you might remember the officer of the Russian Guards who rode with the Prince of Wales and Valentine Baker at the head of the 10th Hussars. I was that officer, and poor Baker was the finest light cavalry officer I ever saw. Had he belonged to us, do you think we should have lost him to the Service he had adorned because of a wretched private folly? Pshaw! What a square-toed, prudish folk you English are! If Valentine Baker could forsake those tatterdemalion Turks and come over the trenches to us, I'll engage the Tzar would make him a full General within a month! Burnaby? Yes, you may see that huge droll fellow as like as not if you go up to the entrenchments. He is quite mad, of course, and always was, and he hates us. But he was my guest at the Mess of the Garde du Corps when he was last in St Petersburg, and our crack giant, old Professor Bakmetieff was not in it with Burnaby either in stature or strength. By George! I'll give you a flag of truce, and if you can persuade Baker and Burnaby to come back and dine with us I shall be delighted beyond measure.'

However, just at that moment, Forbes wrote, 'the mist came down and the army was lost to us.'

The day after Christmas, news reached the Turkish headquarters of a much more ominous kind. Three Russian divisions, freed from the siege at Plevna, were moving up to the head of the Orkhranie Pass. Meanwhile, men and guns were being deployed to the south, quite obviously to surround and cut off any retreat. General Gourko felt he had the whole Turkish army at his mercy.

It was then that Valentine, in his capacity as a General 'Available for Special Purposes' was sent with a scratch division of three thousand men to hold off the massive Russian advance, while the main force under Shakir Pasha attempted to break through the enemy lines and escape through Kamarli and march south to freedom.

Early in the morning of 31 December, while it was still dark, Valentine received news of the impending attack. Accompanied by his staff, Fred Burnaby (still in civilian dress with a bowler hat, pea-jacket, and hessian boots, and carrying a 'stout stick') and Mr Francis Francis, special correspondent of *The Times*, he rode up to a point of vantage above the village of Tashkessan. Through his telescope, despite the early morning mists, he could see the movements of the massive Russian forces, as they advanced slowly through the snow towards the village. Just behind the village was a line of hills, which Valentine had arranged as his first line of defence. The second line, to which he hoped to withdraw later, was immediately behind the first, and he meant to fight every inch of the way. Far away to the north-west, the main Turkish army was waiting for nightfall before they could make their bid for safety.

On the right, a Russian division was advancing along the foot of the mountains – sixteen battalions of Russian Guards were moving towards the centre and had actually reached a point on the Sofia Road. 'By jove, there's a devil of a lot of them!' said Francis. Valentine, putting down his telescope, replied coolly, 'I think we shall be able to account for them yet.'

It was still only seven o'clock in the morning. Shells were already falling from the Russian artillery and one burst only eighty yards from where they stood. Thirty-six guns were counted as firing from the Russian side. The Turks had only five field-guns and two mountain guns. Employing his usual tactics, Valentine had spread out his force, so that it formed a series of detached companies, holding successive hilltops. As the leading Russian brigade advanced, it was met by long-range rifle fire. Suddenly, just as before, the Russian commander halted his division. It seemed too much to hope that they would halt their outflanking movement, so dangerous to Valentine's small force, even if it meant that an immediate attack would follow. But in a few moments, they were advancing to storm the Turkish heights; Valentine ordered his bugler to sound the Turkish battle-cry and in a moment a thousand throats took it up. Burnaby wrote afterwards:

> It was a sensation worth feeling; it was a moment worth ten years of a man's life; and a thrill passed through my heart at the time – that curious sort of thrill, the sensation which you experience when you read of something noble or heroic, or see a gallant action performed. It was grand to hear these two thousand four hundred Mohammedans, many of them raw levies at the time, cheering back in defiance of thirty picked battalions, the choicest troops of the Czar.

As the Russians advanced, the Turks fought bravely, and held each hilltop as long as they dared. It was only in one direction that the defence began to give way. Valentine immediately galloped down the hill and encouraged the men to go forward. He stayed with them for an hour and by the end of that time he had put so much heart into them that they pressed the Russians back. All this time he was under heavy fire but seemed to lead a charmed life.

Gradually he ordered the withdrawal to his second line of hills, defended by four companies of troops based upon an old stone barn which stood on the hillside. Heavy firing broke out all along the line, the Russian Berdan rifles answered by Snider and Martin-Peabody rifles.

They had now been engaged for four hours on the second line of defence. Night could not fall for another three hours and there was still time for Gourko to change his tactics and work round to the flank. Then, to make prospects even blacker, an Aide-de-Camp arrived from the main force under Shakir, saying that they were in full retreat, and advising Valentine to save his men by making an immediate withdrawal. The whole success of the operation had depended on waiting till nightfall, but there was still an hour of daylight left, and the Russians were advancing over the snow.

Valentine once again ordered his trumpeter to sound 'the Battlecry' to his tired troops. With a shout of 'Allah!' the wiry Bosnians sprang to their feet and dashed forward in a bayonet-charge against the legendary Russian Guard. The famous Guard wavered, and then retreated headlong down the heights. At dusk, the fire had died out all along the line. The Turkish soldiers climbed on the rocks, waved their weapons and cheered. Valentine knew that he had accomplished all that he had hoped in that single day. The main Turkish army under Shakir had escaped from the Russian pincer movement and was in full retreat towards Adrianople. It now only remained for him to follow.

The War Office historian, Captain Hosier, was to write later:

'It would be difficult to find in all records of history, whether ancient or modern, a more brilliant act of military heroism.'

The story of the retreat that followed, through the Rhodope mountains to the Aegean Sea, was a story of hardship and suffering for the troops. Valentine insisted on travelling with the fifth brigade at the rear, blowing up a vital bridge only after the cavalry had thundered over it.

Many acts of unselfish heroism were recorded, and all the while Burnaby was at his side. Valentine wrote later, 'My good friend Captain Burnaby used to watch over me like a child, and was always ready with some sustenance that might prevent my health from failing. . . .'

After a month of almost continual marching, always pursued and harassed by the Russians, Valentine wrote:

> 'We were down to our last rations, and unless we could reach the plain within the next two days, we would all die of exposure and exhaustion. My little grey horse, which I had purchased in Sofia and which I had ridden continuously in the campaign, proved a perfect treasure during this trying march, in spite of the shortage of fodder which affected all the horses. The men were worn and weary with their trying marches day after day through snow and ice, but they now felt that the end of their difficulties was approaching. After the final summit had been surmounted, the soldiers had halted, and an excited cry went up from all sides – 'The sea – the sea!'

The long march was over, and the Aegean Sea lay below them shining and sparkling in the sunshine.

The next day the army was to embark for Gallipoli, but Valentine and Burnaby were both distressed to see no sign of the Royal Navy. In fact, on 23 January, only the day before, the Fleet had entered the Dardanelles, but the order had been countermanded from London. In a few hours, the Fleet had retired to Besika Bay.

The whole situation in Constantinople had been in a state of continuous crisis for weeks. In December, the British Ambassador, Layard, had written that the end was approaching for Turkey unless England came to her help.* The Queen herself sent a memorandum to the Cabinet on 12 January, reminding them that it had already been decided that a threat to Constantinople would free England from any obligation to neutrality. 'If those were merely empty words' she said, 'England would sink to a third-rate power.'

However, the Grand Duke Nicholas, who commanded the forces advancing on Constantinople, informed the Porte that there could be no armistice until the basis of peace was determined. In the meantime, while the terms were under discussion, the Russians continued to advance. . . .

On arriving at Constantinople, Burnaby and Valentine found that the recent reports of the Russian advance had caused a ferment in the city.

---

* Account from the report by Sir Henry Layard.

The Sultan, convinced that his life was in danger, had even asked Layard secretly if he could have asylum for himself and his family, and the gunboat *Antelope* was made ready. Valentine wrote:

> We had now for a long time been without any political news from the outside world, but it seemed to me essential that the danger which now threatened both Constantinople and the Dardanelles so severely must lead to immediate action from England. The importance of Gallipoli as giving an opening for that action was so apparent, that I looked to the security of this port with intense anxiety. Should Gallipoli fall and the Dardanelles be occupied by the Russians, the action of England must be completely cramped, and Constantinople would fall an easy prey to Russia. So unsatisfactory were the preparations for the defence of Constantinople that I immediately made a report to the Turkish Authorities on the subject.

Valentine pointed out to Sulieman the absolute necessity of immediately strengthening Gallipoli, and, in fact, he was given 'Carte Blanche' to do so.

With his previous knowledge of the country around Constantinople and the Sea of Marmora, he would have been the ideal commander to have strengthened the defences, but just at that moment, news filtered through to him, from a newspaper correspondent, that in the absence of communication with the capital, the Army had agreed to new terms imposed by the Russians. The terms were that the Russians were to advance, while the Turkish Army was to withdraw. . . .

Valentine wrote:

> I cannot attempt to describe the profound and painful impression made upon me by this abandonment of the line of defence with which I had been so intimately associated. I paid a visit to Raouff Pasha early on the following morning. He was greatly depressed, and confirmed the news.
>
> Utterly disgusted, and determined not to be a witness of the unnecessary retreat of the Turkish Army, I requested immediate permission to return to England on leave of absence and started for London via Brindisi on the following afternoon.

13

'NO COMMON PERSON'

On his return to England, Valentine was to find a very different atmosphere from that which he had left only a year before. The massacres which had been described so vividly in Gladstone's pamphlet *Bulgarian Horrors* were now succeeded by other reports of Turkish sufferings at Russian hands as they pressed on towards Constantinople. The threat of a Russian advance had always haunted the British people since the war in the Crimea and now the majority of the country was 'up in arms'.

The Queen had written to the Prime Minister, saying she would not remain Sovereign of a country 'that is letting itself down to kiss the feet of the great barbarians, the retarders of all civilisation and liberty that exist. Oh, if the Queen were a man, she would like to go and give these Russians, whose word one cannot believe, such a beating.'

Lord Beaconsfield had, however, failed to win over the Cabinet to more positive action to halt the Russian advance. The word Jingo-ism dates from this time, and the music-hall song –

We don't want to fight
But by jingo if we do
We've got the men, we've got the ships
We've got the money too.

showed a wave of patriotic fervour which was sweeping the country.

Valentine, just back from the centre of activity, was of course able to offer invaluable advice to the Prime Minister.

★ ★ ★

While Valentine was in England, the Treaty of Stefano was signed on 3 March, after careful negotiations. Although this effectively halted the Russian advance on Constantinople, Great Britain and Austro-Hungary could still not agree on terms. As in 1876, two years earlier, Valentine's advice was sought yet again.

In a letter from 10 Downing Street, Lord Beaconsfield wrote to the Queen:

> With my humble duty to Your Majesty.
> The Cabinet discussed to-day Count Andrassy's new proposals, and agreed to press him for more detailed descriptions of his wishes and intentions.
>
> At present he offers us nothing and wants a great deal which no House of Commons would grant. Indeed he offers neither co-operation nor security. However, we keep negotiations alive. Lord Beaconsfield has had a long interview with Baker Pasha this morning. He is a first-rate man, and, in the event of War, may play a great figure and accomplish vast service.
>
> He is a complete master of his subject and should be at the head of a Turkish Contingent of 50,000 men. His views are deep, yet precise; no common person.

Valentine was only to stay a few months in England and returned to Constantinople soon afterwards to resume his duties with the Turkish Army. Still in the rank of Lieutenant-General, he was given the task of regrouping the Army and was, once again, given permission to reinforce the lines around Constantinople itself. He was also asked to carry out such military reforms as he thought to be necessary.

It was a three-fold appointment for which his capabilities were eminently suited. He was to remain in Turkey for the next two years carrying out these tasks, and was soon to be promoted to the post of Military Adviser to the Ottoman Empire.

Meanwhile, in the summer following the signing of the Treaty of San Stefano, on 18 May, the Russians, without warning, moved their front line forward. Valentine again advised the Government at home, that he thought that an attack on Constantinople might be imminent. Fortunately a wiser course than heretofore was now taken in London. Lord Salisbury had succeeded Lord Derby at the Foreign Office and, less than a month later, on 13 June, the outcome of negotiations brought about the now famous Congress of Berlin.

This was the most important gathering of diplomats since the Congress of Vienna in 1815. Bulgaria, the main bone of contention, was tri-sected, reducing the power of Russia, whilst the Turks were given the benefit of the Balkan barrier once more.

Austro-Hungary received the right to administer the controversial countries of Bosnia, Herzegovina and Montenegro. Lord Beaconsfield returned to England in triumph. He had brought back 'Peace with Honour' and the enormous aggrandisement of Russia, so wisely foreseen by Valentine was, for the time being at least, halted.

During the next two years, Valentine's name became something of a legend in England. Only returning very rarely, he threw himself into the re-organisation of the Turkish Army. He was known as General Valentine Baker Pasha, and was spoken of as a romantic and mysterious figure, much as Lawrence of Arabia was described during the next century. That his qualities were very much respected is shown in letters from Lord Salisbury to Sir Henry Layard, still the British Ambassador in Constantinople.

He wrote early in 1879, 'Sir Henry Layard speaks hopefully of obtaining the appointment of General Baker to a high military post in Kurdistan. Of the advantage of such a selection there can be no question – but I feel very little confidence of its being effected.'

Valentine was not, in fact, offered an appointment, but, in his position as Military Adviser to the Ottoman Empire, there was proof that he had the confidence, not only of our discerning Ambassador, but of the Sultan. Meanwhile his good friend Fred Burnaby amused himself by flinging himself into politics, standing for Birmingham, where he was defeated by Joseph Chamberlain, and then lightheartedly crossing the Channel by balloon.

EGYPT: 'THE BRAVEST SOLDIER ENGLAND EVER HAD'

14

DEPRIVED OF COMMAND

After the Congress of Berlin the danger of war in the Middle East had temporarily receded, but an ever more complicated problem now presented itself to the British Government.

In 1882, the situation in Egypt can only be described as chaotic. Sam Baker, who had retired from his Governorship of the Sudan in 1875, watched with growing alarm from his home in Devonshire as it became ever more apparent that disaffection was spreading throughout the Sudan.

For many years, under the benign rule of the Porte's representative, the Khedive Ismail, Egypt and the Sudan had prospered, in spite of the terrors of the slave trade and the duplicity of many of the Khedive's officials. Sam Baker and General Charles Gordon, who succeeded him as Governor General of the Sudan, had both expressed loyalty and admiration for Ismail, the highlight of whose rule was, perhaps, the construction of the Suez Canal by de Lesseps, which was finally opened in 1869.

Nothing could have exceeded the grandeur of the opening of the Canal. Three pavilions were built at Port Said – the pyramids were illuminated with magnesium light, and the whole of Cairo was *en fête*.

The climax of the day was when the Empress Eugénie of France herself, a cousin of de Lesseps, sailed in her yacht *L'aigle* before the fleet of following ships through the Canal for the first time. Egypt had prospered but Ismail, always wildly extravagant, had vastly overspent his resources.

Only six years later, Disraeli, with the help of Baron Rothschild, had been able to purchase the Khedive's Suez Canal shares for four million pounds. The Queen was delighted by this visionary move on Disraeli's part, and he had been created a baron in the following year, although Gladstone remained deeply critical of him to the end of his life.

A condominium was formed between the British and French, originally created for the payment by Egypt of the interest on her huge debt, but it meant that, effectively, the British and French representatives almost ran the country.

The impoverished Khedive decided to call a Conference in 1878. General Gordon, Lord Dufferin (who had come over from Constantinople where he had succeeded Layard as our Ambassador) and de Lesseps were invited, but Gordon left in disgust after two days and the Conference broke down.

After this, Ismail, making a hopeless effort to break away from foreign intervention, dismissed the European representatives and, for a short while, managed to survive.

He even thought it wise to include one, Arabi, in his Government, who was perhaps one of the most forthright young officers in the Egyptian Army, and whose slogan was 'Egypt for the Egyptians'.

It was soon after this that the British and French influence in the Porte persuaded the Sultan, his master, to telegraph Ismail as the 'Ex-Khedive of Egypt'. Ismail retired to his yacht on the Bosphorus, and his son, Tewfik, succeeded to the monumental debts, the restless Army and the unsteady throne of his father. It was soon after the deposition of Ismail that, imperceptibly at first, the problem of Egypt and the Sudan became of even more vital importance to the British Government, for there rose up, without at first attracting much attention in Cairo, a remarkable religious and militant leader, Mahommed Ahmed-ibn-el Sayyid Abdullah, or 'The Mahdi'. Still without causing any very great stir in Egypt, the desert tribes began to flock to his banner.

The revolt that he led was at first ignored, partly because, after General Gordon had left, there was no-one in Cairo who really understood the problem of the Sudan; and secondly, because a second revolt in February, 1881, in Egypt itself, by the Egyptian Army, now under the leadership of Arabi, concerned the Government in England far more.

Arabi seized the government buildings in Cairo almost without opposition. Tewfik gave in without a battle and guns and fortifications were put up on the sea wall at Alexandria. Fifty Europeans were massacred in the rising, and many hundreds tried to leave the country.

On 22 June, despite his principles of non-involvement, Gladstone, now Prime Minister, felt compelled to ask the Commons for the necessary vote in support of an Expeditionary Force. Meanwhile, a fleet under Admiral Sir Beauchamp Seymour moved in.

The Admiral sent an ultimatum to Arabi, saying that unless work on the batteries ceased immediately, he would fire on the city. Work proceeded and he opened his bombardment. Arabi and his followers fled. The bombardment was followed by immediate support from the British Army under General Sir Garnet Wolseley, resulting in the complete victory of Tel-el-Kebir, the Egyptian Army having fled in wild confusion.

It was after that victory that the Egyptian Army under Arabi was completely disbanded. A few weeks later, Lord Dufferin was sent once more on a special mission to Cairo, to 'advise the Government of the Khedive on the arrangements that would have to be made for re-establishing his Highness' authority'. Lord Dufferin recommended that the Egyptian Army should be entirely reorganised under the command of a British general.

Sir Garnet Wolseley immediately proposed Lieutenant General Valentine Baker Pasha for the post. He set great store by the qualities of military leadership which he knew Valentine to possess. So it was that on Wolseley's commendation and the support of the Prince of Wales and the Duke of Cambridge, the appointment was offered to Valentine by the Khedive.

★ ★ ★

During the past few years the Prince of Wales had again pleaded with the Queen for Valentine's restoration. On 2 December 1879, Lord Ponsonby had referred to one such request in a letter to the Duke of Cambridge:

> Sir, I have the honour of receiving his Royal Highness' letters, and communicating them to the Queen.
>
> The Prince of Wales was very anxious I should inform your Royal Highness that he had communicated to the Queen a request from Baker Pasha for restoration to the British Army. The Queen is by no means favourable to this proceeding, but if the Ministers insist on it as an absolute necessity will not oppose it. But Her Majesty will not receive him at Court.
>
> I do not understand in what manner Baker Pasha desires to be restored.
>
> Ponsonby.

It had not been a very encouraging letter. Meanwhile Fred Burnaby had been tireless in praise of his friend, since his return to England. At a dinner at the Savage Club, he had given such a glowing account of Valentine's achievements at Tashkashen that he had been re-elected to the Army and Navy Club. Burnaby had also applied, through Lady Ely,

Queen Victoria's Lady-in-Waiting, for his re-instatement in the British Army.

But it had all been to no avail.

Now, at last, it seemed that the past would be forgotten, and Valentine Baker would be able to take his place once more in the service of his Sovereign.

15

A COURAGEOUS DECISION

One can imagine with what torn feelings Valentine faced the decision now placed before him. For he had gained a position of great responsibility and even greater respect in Constantinople, yet, at the same time, he greeted the news of the Khedive's invitation with a thrill of anticipation and accepted the appointment.

Now, at last, he could take up a command ideally suited to his talents, for he knew he could create an Army in Egypt, an army led by British officers, which would be second to none in efficiency and achievement.

It was an added delight that his wife, Fanny and his two young daughters, could join him among the English community in Egypt. There were quite a number of British residents in Cairo and Alexandria, although, as we have seen, many had decided to leave for home at the time of the bombardment. The family could stay at Shepheard's Hotel, while looking for a house, or with the popular English community at Gezira. At last they could now live together as a family, after seven long years of continuous separation.

Valentine's hopes were high as he took ship for Port Said from Constantinople, and soon his tall figure was to be seen riding through the streets of Cairo on a beautiful grey Arab, past the eucalyptus trees and the palm trees lining the wide dusty roads of the capital.

These roads were usually crowded with heavily-laden donkeys and tall dignified camels, swaying along under their heavy loads, and often led by one small boy, holding a red or blue cord attached to their halters. Everything was astir in the capital – the long white 'djallabah' contrasting with red tarbouches in the markets and the black 'yashmaks' of the women, with their decoration of beads and small coins.

For two months Valentine threw himself into the organisation of the new Army. He proposed to include troops from Turkey and Albania to strengthen the now scattered and demoralised Egyptian soldiers, and hoped, on the advice of his brother Sam, to include a Sudanese battalion, as Sir Samuel had known them to be splendid fighters when he was facing the cruel slave-traders south of Khartoum.

Valentine naturally applied for British officers to train the troops, and it was then that he was to receive yet another very bitter blow. To his consternation his request was refused.

The request for British officers to serve under him had sparked off the old question as to whether he should be re-instated in the British Army, as it was not possible for British officers to serve under someone who had been cashiered. Lord Dufferin, who knew Valentine well in Constantinople, at length stepped in with a compromise, but it was a compromise which did nothing to cure the wound which Valentine must have felt.

The following letters show the course of events. The first, from Lord Ponsonby to the Prince of Wales refers to a letter from Lord Dufferin to the Queen.

Windsor Castle,
November 27 1882

General Sir Henry Ponsonby humbly begs leave to say that this proposal of Lord Dufferin's may possibly solve the difficulty as regards *Baker Pasha*.

According to his own account, as given in the letter from Baker Pasha to Mr. Knollys, he accepted the post of Commander-in-Chief of the Egyptian Army with the approval of Mr. Gladstone and Lord Granville.

But when he asked for eighty officers on full pay to serve in the Army the Duke of Cambridge and Mr Childers pointed out that it was impossible for these officers to be under the command of one who had been expelled from the Army.

If Baker Pasha is placed at the head of the Gendarmerie the same objection could not apply.

The Prince of Wales himself was to write two letters on December 3rd: the first was to Mr. Gladstone imploring him to relent. He wrote:

It is not for me to comment on the decision of the Cabinet, but I must confess I think Baker Pasha has been very hardly and unfairly treated. To deprive him now of the important command, which the Khedive conferred upon him, is simply to ruin him.

On the same day, he begged Lord Wolseley to intercede with the Government and not allow his friend to 'fall between two stools'. But it was all to no avail. On 6 December, this letter was followed by a long letter from Lord Granville, the Foreign Secretary, to the Prince of Wales.

December 4th 1882

To the Prince of Wales from Lord Granville:

Sir, I spoke to Mr. Gladstone this afternoon on the subject of the letter which your Royal Highness has done me the honour to write on the subject of Baker Pasha.

He told me he had already spoken to your Royal Highness, and, finding that I had also heard from you, he asked me to state for you the principal points of the case.

We never invited Baker Pasha to go to Egypt – we did not commit ourselves to any appointment for him there. We constantly insisted and as often received the promise, that no plans should be discussed without our previous knowledge and sanction, and were surprised to find that he had been appointed and had agreed to be Commander-in-Chief of the Army, without our having been informed of the fact.

The Khedive and the Egyptian Government have expressed an opinion that the appointment of English officers is a necessity. All the authorities agree that if this is so, they should be taken from the active and not from the retired list. The Cabinet were of the same opinion as Mr. Childers, that it would be impossible to place English officers under the command of one who had been dismissed from the British Army, and I informed Lord Dufferin of the final decision of the Cabinet to this effect.

Lord Dufferin recommended that Colonel Baker should be appointed to the command of the Gendarmerie, and to this Her Majesty's Government has agreed.

I can understand the disappointment of Baker Pasha at having lost the Commander-in-Chief of the Army, and he appears to me to have claims to a position equal to that which (he) held in Turkey, but this seems to have been denied him.

I greatly regret it being out of my power to meet your Royal Highness' wishes, but it would be impossible for me to reverse the instructions which (were) based on a final decision of the Cabinet.

I have the honour to be, Sir,
With profound respect,
Your Royal Highness' humble servant,
Granville.

In face of the Cabinet's decision, the Prince of Wales could do no more. Two days later the Duke of Connaught was writing to the Queen.

Bagshot Park,
Surrey.
December 6th 1882

Dearest Mamma,

I thank you for your kind letter and hasten to return Lord Dufferin's interesting letter. I am very glad that Baker Pasha is going to command in the Soudan; he is an excellent officer, understands Easterns well, and I think has been rather badly treated by the Government who at first quite approved of his coming to Egypt to command their army . . .

It was obvious that Valentine Baker had given up his command at Constantinople under a most cruel misapprehension, but with typical courage, and all the vigour and skill at his command, he now set himself the task of reorganising the Gendarmerie.

The Gendarmerie he had now to command had now been divested of its military status and was removed from the War Ministry to the Ministry of the Interior. It was, for the most part, as described by Sir Samuel Baker, to be composed of 'those native fellaheen who hated a military life, and were emasculated as a fighting force – their idea of battle was a quick retreat'.

It must have been a very sad day when Valentine Baker heard that the new Egyptian Army was to be put in the hands of General Sir Evelyn Wood.

Young British officers were now engaged to help in the training of the troops. Among those young officers were Reginald Wingate [later to become Sir Reginald] and a young Captain, named Kitchener.

★   ★   ★

It was in April that Captain Wingate arrived in Cairo from India, where he had been serving in the Royal Artillery as a battery commander. He had quite suddenly received a letter from Sir Evelyn Wood, offering him an appointment in the new Egyptian army.

On 4 June, Wingate, his groom and an Arab pony landed at Suez. There was some talk of putting the pony in quarantine, but, instead, he gave it a bath in the presence of the Egyptian authorities, and this seemed to suffice! He started the next day by train for Cairo via Ismailia, arriving the next afternoon. He at once paid his respects to the Khedive, Tewfik, and afterwards met both General Valentine Baker and also young Captain Kitchener. It was then that he wrote:

Valentine Baker had commanded the Tenth Hussars, but had had to resign his commission owing to a scandal in which, in fact, he was the innocent party, and he was seeking his future under the Khedive.

At this time Valentine, Fanny and their two young daughters, Hermione and Sybil, were living in some comfort in a *diahbeah*, or large houseboat, on the Nile. The cousin of whom Fanny was so fond, Fanny Wormald, often stayed with them, and was invaluable in helping in any illness or emergency.

Both Wingate and Kitchener were fascinated by Valentine's elder daughter, Hermione, now a beautiful young girl of sixteen, but unfortunately, she had never been very strong, and the exhausting Egyptian summer had not suited her, and she had become very delicate. Valentine was utterly devoted to her and both he and Fanny were continually anxious about her health.

A cholera epidemic broke out among the troops in the summer, and Wingate was found to be suffering from the illness, after he had worked untiringly building special isolation camps for the victims. He was sent home to England on 16 September, and on his return was decorated with the 4th Class Order of the Osmanie in appreciation of his work – a great honour for so young a soldier.

So it was that during the long hot summer it was usually Captain Kitchener who visited General Valentine Baker in his *diahbeah*. He had first met Valentine in Bulgaria in 1877 and had much admired his heroic stand against the Russian advance. He now became a frequent visitor, and very soon it was said that he had fallen in love with the lovely Hermione. However, owing to the delicate state of her health and her youth, they had decided not to announce their engagement until later.

It was not only a family story. A friend, Bonte Elgood, when a little girl of only ten years old, was taken by her mother to visit Hermione at Shepherd's Hotel with some beef-tea. As her mother was about to go into the Bakers' apartment, a good-looking young man came out. Her mother immediately told her that they could not visit Hermione that afternoon as she was with her young man, Kitchener, whom she was going to marry*.

Lady Twining, a cousin, also confirmed the story, and said that Kitchener always wore a gold locket, containing a portrait of Hermione. She had been told this by Hermione's younger sister, Sybil.

---

* From Sir Philip Magnus *Kitchener, Architect of Victory* (Published by William Kimber) This letter can be seen in the Records Office.

Meanwhile, the threat by the Mahdi was growing in the Sudan. On the very day that Alexandria had been bombarded, the Mahdi had conquered El Obeid, the capital of Kordofan, and had found himself in possession of the an enormous quantity of guns and ammunition stored in the city. From then on his fame spread, and the Chiefs began flocking to his banner.

It seemed to Sir Samuel Baker, for he was at that time back in Cairo with his wife, that action must be taken immediately to retain Sennar, the province to the East of Khartoum, for without the rich grain from Sennar, Khartoum could not survive. It was hopeless to expect help from Gladstone, or indeed from the newly-formed Egyptian Army. They were under training and not ready for action in the field.

The Khedive, Tewfik, then asked Valentine if he could recommend a leader, and it was arranged that Colonel Hicks, from the Bombay Army, should collect a force and move towards Khartoum, but on no account should they cross over to the Western Bank. This was emphasised by both Sam and Valentine – Sam acting as adviser to his brother. At first the expedition was entirely successful, and the forces of the Mahdi were driven back. However, disastrously, Hicks' orders were then changed by the Minister of War in Cairo. Sam wrote:

> The control of the Sudan had been placed in the hands of the Minister of War in Cairo, having been removed from General V. Baker's department in the process of the new organisation. Elated by the success of Abd-el-Kedar and Colonel Hicks' operations in Sennar, orders were now issued by the Egyptian Minister in direct opposition to those which had been so carefully adhered to . . . Hicks was to re-conquer Kordofan and Dafur! [on the western side of the Nile]
>
> An officer who was utterly ignorant of Arabic, with an English staff equally uninformed, was to be sent into the deserts of Kordofan with an army of eleven or twelve thousand men, all of whom were suspicious of Englishmen, who were in occupation of Egypt proper and none of whom could be depended on in any great emergency . . . When I heard this astounding news I could only utter the word 'Destruction'.*

It was a terrible disaster. Years later, a leather diary, in Arabic, written by an Egyptian officer in Hicks' force, Abbas Bey, came into

---

*From 'African Development in the Sudan', an article hitherto unpublished by Sir Samuel Baker

Wingate's possession. This describes in detail the terrible last six weeks' march of the doomed expedition, from its start on the Nile to within two days of its final destruction.

But it was not only Khartoum and Kordofan which were causing anxiety in Cairo. A supporter of the Mahdi, Osman Digna, had invaded Sinkat, Trinkitat and Tokar, on the borders of the Suez Canal.

At Trinkitat, Captain Moncrieff, the British Consul at Jeddah, had been killed, and in all three places the Egyptian forces were annihilated, almost to a man. Suakin, the Red Sea Port, was directly threatened by the rebels. It was realised that its loss would not only be serious for Egypt, but would have repercussions on the safety of the Red Sea Route, so vital to England for her communications with India.

This series of disasters raised a storm in the Press both in England and in Cairo. Something had to be done, but still the British Government had taken no steps to meet the crisis.

The general with the most brilliant record, General Valentine Baker, had been denied control of the Egyptian Army, but he was in Cairo, and he was under the control of the Egyptian Ministry of War. It was on 27 November, only one week after the news of the disaster of the Hicks' expedition reached Cairo and was confirmed that the Khedive sent for Valentine Baker. He asked him if, with his Gendarmerie, he would relieve the garrisons of Tokar and Trinkitat.

Sir Reginald Wingate (as he would become) was to write later:

> At the same time, with a perversity almost unknown in British History, so soon after the terrible fate of the Hicks' expedition, General Valentine Baker was sent off with as ill-equipped an army as it would be possible to find, consisting of the Egyptian Gendarmerie who were unused to fighting anyway, to relieve Sinkat and protect Suakin.

On 28 November, Sam, now home at Sandford Orleigh, wrote hastily to his brother:

> I see that they [the Egyptians] have fallen back on the Gendarmerie as their only available force! I also see that men but not their officers, have refused to proceed to the Sudan. Let nothing persuade you to attempt the passage of the Suakin Desert with such troops otherwise you will share the fate of Hicks . . .

But the letter was too late to influence his brother, who left for Suakin on 15 December.

The following extracts from a contemporary private diary, written in Cairo by Fanny Wormald, who was staying with the Bakers just before the start of the expedition, gives a very vivid picture of the chaotic state of affairs in the capital at that time, and how the vast enterprise of relieving the garrisons at Tokar and Trinkitat, was so hurriedly and unwisely undertaken:

November 25 1883
Val is overwhelmed with work, in consequence of this terrible disaster to Hicks in the Sudan. He looks thin and ill, and is very anxious about Hermione.

November 27th
On Sunday strong pressure was put upon Val to go to Suakin – he was most depressed having to leave his daughter at the crisis of her illness. He saw the Khedive at ten o'clock, and of course said he would go. The Khedive told him he 'was deeply touched by his devotion'. There was work all day; and at 5 pm he managed to rush home. The sitting-room was then besieged with officers. At seven o'clock, a Turkish officer (afterwards killed at El Teb) dashed in to say that the Turks, to a man, had refused to march. Everyone had hoped that the Turks would have acted as a backbone to the invertebrate Egyptian troops. It was a terrible blow! 'Oh that I should have lived to see this day!' exclaimed the Turk, after making his report.

Val said 'I would give a great deal, if I could make a good speech in Turkish' whereupon an officer remarked 'I will find you an eloquent person'. Val sent for this 'eloquent person' and went at once to harangue the troops. We saw him no more until midnight, when he returned to tell us the result.

This is what happened. First, the Turkish troops explained their case. They had been engaged to remain in Egypt Proper; and they would fulfil their contract and defend Egypt to the last man – but they would not go to the Sudan. This was quite true, as Val told us. They were all married men; and the British Authorities had insisted on their serving as civilians, not as a regular arm of the service. The 'eloquent person' then addressed them: but his exhortation fell flat. The Turkish officers then addressed their men, with the same result. Finally, Val spoke to them, saying he knew the Turks were brave, and he could not believe that his own men were cowards. 'I myself must go' he added, 'Shall I go alone?'

There was a pause, during which Val thought that he too had failed to make an impression; 'I'll give you five minutes to think it over,' he exclaimed, 'the brave men will fall in on the right; the cowards on the left.'

A handsome Bosnian, not one of the Egyptians, at once went over to the right; then two or three more, then a good many. Then, those who had first crossed over, rushed back to the ranks, and seized the hands of their special friends among the waverers, pulling them forcibly towards the right; until more than half were ranged upon the 'brave' side. The remainder were allowed the night for reflection.

Fanny felt very sad, and begged Val not to go; but he reassured her saying, 'Wood (Sir Evelyn, Commander-in-Chief) will forward supplies'. All sorts of promises had been made to Val. 'They have given me "*carte blanche*"', he said, 'But' his wife rejoined, 'what is the good of "*carte blanche*" if you have troops without courage?' . . . . On Monday night, Val said, as if thinking aloud, 'I wish Burnaby were here! He shall know this.'

The diary continues:

December 15th

To-day we saw a long line of '*miserables*' chained together – recruits for the Egyptian army!

The Barings are most kind. Sir Evelyn will, we think, see that food and fodder are sent to Suakin, for starvation is one of the perils of the expedition. It is a comfort to think that Colonel Burnaby is to arrive shortly.

Val had to leave by an early train tonight; and Luigi was determined that the last dinner should be tempting. There were no guests; and we were trying whether we could decipher and write the code by which we were to communicate, when Zubeir Pasha was announced. Zubeir was the great slave trader whose son Suleiman, Gordon's lieutenant, Gessi, had killed.

We knew how anxious Val was to have this notorious Arab with him, his influence with the tribes being at that time very great. It was etiquette for the ladies to retire at once but, as we left the room, we glanced back with interest at Zubeir and his staff. His appearance was striking. His high-caste Arab features and slight angular frame contrasted with his dusky complexion. The interview was most friendly. To our surprise, also, he appeared at the station, and assured F that he hoped soon to join her husband, where he would 'watch over his safety'.

But Zubeir, probably after a stormy interview with General Gordon in January, failed to keep his promise. The diary continues:

The enthusiasm at the station, in which even the natives took part, was a popular ovation that has never been surpassed here. There was an enormous crowd, and all were deeply stirred by the leave-taking.

In a letter to her cousin, Fanny Wormald described Valentine's departure in even more detail. She wrote:

The station and approaches were so crammed with people and carriages that crowds of his own friends could not get in at all. General Grenfell was one who did manage it, and said to him: 'Every officer in my Brigade is here, but as they cannot get to you to bid you goodbye I do so for them, and they request me to let you know how proud they will all be to serve under you, they hope at no distant date.'

All Cairo seemed to be at the station, although it was late at night. Val's special train did not move off till 11 pm amidst cheers. They say he looked excited, and happy, for the darling of his heart (Hermione) was better. Hermione had improved for two or three days.

They only told her of his journey the day before, and made as light of it as possible. She thinks he has only gone for a fortnight to look after the State of Suakin.

Val went to her at his usual hour of 8 in the evening, and when he left the house after 10, the Nurse was waiting outside Hermione's door and whispered that she was sleeping calmly.

All the rest of the party went to the station. The illness, and having to leave her had been a great trial to him.*

And so Valentine Baker left for Suakin.

---

* Original letter in the possession of the Baker family.

16

SUAKIN AND THE BATTLE OF EL TEB

Meanwhile, in London, General Gordon was recalled from Palestine by the Government, and a series of letters to Sam describe the agonising decision he had to make, for he had already agreed to go out to the Congo with Stanley, under the King of the Belgians.

On 4 January, he wrote from Brussels with a suggestion that Sir Samuel himself might go out once more as Civil Governor of the Sudan, while General Valentine Baker Pasha should command the Army. It was a brilliant suggestion, but, just beforehand, on 1 January, Sam had written to *The Times* with his own suggestion that General Gordon should be Governor.

It was on 8 January, only a few days after writing his letter, that Gordon arrived at Southampton from Belgium, and stayed the night with his sister. The very next day he was amazed to find that the editor of the Pall Mall Gazette, Mr W.T. Head, had travelled down from London to interview him. On 10 January, an account of the interview, a full page report and a leading article appeared in the Gazette, reporting his views on the Sudan.

From then on there was tremendous pressure from the newspapers and the public that Gordon should go out to Khartoum.

It is interesting to note, however, from papers and letters still kept in the Baker family, how nearly Sam went out in his stead. For after the interview with the Pall Mall Gazette, Gordon decided to stay with Sam Baker at Sandford Orleigh in Devon to discuss the matter.

Sam's daughter, Ettie, recalled that Gordon was met at the station by her father. During the drive up to the house Gordon almost persuaded Sam to go in his stead. At first Sam's imagination was fired by the idea. He could speak the language, while Gordon could not: he knew the country as well as his visitor – he almost felt that he should go. But on arrival at the house, his beautiful second wife, Florence, 'put her foot down'. She said he had promised they should not go out to the Sudan again together, and it was unthinkable that he should go alone.

Sam looked at General Gordon as much as to say 'You see how it is!'

Gordon was upset, and very silent at dinner, but Ettie described his 'magnetic blue eyes'.

So Gordon left for Khartoum on 18 January. He arrived at Charing Cross Station at 8 am, accompanied by his Military Assistant, Colonel Hamill Stewart, late of the 11th Hussars, who was travelling with him. There the farewell party included the Duke of Cambridge himself, Lord Stanhope and General Sir Garnet Wolseley.

At the last moment Gordon realised that he had very little money, and Wolseley hastily pressed three hundred gold sovereigns into his hand, just before the train steamed out of the station.

It was the last time they were ever to see General Gordon. From Cyprus, a postcard reached Sir Samuel Baker:

> Under no circumstances will Government guarantee future – the only thing is to get Sudan to settle down.

He was told simply to 'Relieve the Garrison at Khartoum', with no military support from the Gladstone Government. He did not know, until after his appointment, that 'abandonment' was the Government's policy. He had already in fact expressed himself freely, in opposition to the idea. He had been quoted in the Pall Mall Gazette:

> It was all very well to talk about evacuation, but such talk was not practicable. Whatever you decide, you cannot evacuate, because your army cannot be moved. You must either surrender absolutely to the Mahdi, or defend Khartoum at all hazards.

The news of General Gordon's departure was at first greeted with great enthusiasm, but the step had no sooner been taken than the politicians wavered – his instructions were never confirmed.

Gordon was to write later to Gladstone when he was besieged in Khartoum: 'I altogether decline the imputation that the projected expedition has come up to relieve *me*. It has come up to save our National Honour.'

Meanwhile, in Cairo, the expedition under Valentine had left for Suakin on 15 December to relieve Tokar and Sinkat. He was given a force of 450 Turkish and Egyptian cavalry, 1500 assorted black troops, and 1000 of his Gendarmerie who were only under contract to serve in Egypt and had no wish to fight. Osman Digna, the Mahdi's principal commander, on the other hand, had over 20,000 picked and dedicated fighting men in the Field.

On 3 December, in London, Fred Burnaby received a telegram from Fanny Baker. It ran 'V says do come if you can'. A few days later he received the following letter:

Dear Colonel Burnaby,

I have just sent you a telegram by Val's wish. He does so hope that you may feel inclined to come out here at once, for the situation is most exciting and he feels very strongly that no-one would be more interested in the state of things, or be so valuable a friend and helper as you.

I need not go into the long story of how, when the crisis arrived, it was discovered that the much-vaunted Egyptians could by no means be sent to fight, but that Val and his 'Police' must be sent off at once. You will have *some* idea of these things from the newspapers, but I do not suppose things have been fully telegraphed home, for certain people have got such an iron hand over the Press that none of the correspondents dare send unbiased telegrams. . . . I am really terrified about Val's chances. Of course whenever there is a chance of fighting I am always very much frightened, but hitherto I have always been able to think of him as surrounded by brave soldiers who would follow him anywhere. Now he is to go to Suakin with a set of untried people, about whom we know only *one* thing – that cowardice is their nature, and with such tools there, and an obstructive person *here* in his own office this prospect does seem to me gloomy indeed.

We are longing for you. It is impossible to get anyone here to telegraph facts as they are. I suppose that when this letter reaches England you may be on your way here, but in case you are obliged to remain at home *could* you talk to some of the leading Press people? I wonder if they know what an utter farce 'liberty of the Press' is here . . . It is as if last winter's injustices have started up under a fresh dress!! This is a long letter, but Val may not have time to write, he is busy all day long and we both long for your help and sympathy.

I am sorry to tell that my poor girl has had two relapses, she is dreadfully weak and makes slow progress. She is, however, better to-day.

Believe me, dear Colonel Burnaby,
Yours very sincerely,
Fanny Baker.

This letter shows Fanny's acute anxiety and also here confidence in Burnaby. Her appeal was answered at once. On 20 January 1884,

Burnaby, having obtained extended leave from his Regiment, set off for Suakin. Meanwhile Valentine had arrived with his straggling force. But the promised supplies never arrived.

On 8 January, Valentine wrote:

Suakin, 8th January 1884
They have sent down nothing, no boats, no telegraph, no Turks, no anything! Nor have I any news of Zubeir's men. The telegraph I want above all things, and you know the promises that were made about all the matters – it really is too bad! On the other hand, it is quite refreshing to have such a man as Admiral Hewett here, he is the personification of kindness, hospitality and straightforwardness ... I am getting on rather better with the friendly chiefs; but Sinkat and Tokar are a source of great anxiety, for what can I do for them if I get no support from Cairo?

Fanny Wormald's diary, written in Cairo, now continues:

January 28th, Cairo.
We have had an exciting week. Colonel Harrington came from Suakin to hasten up men and supplies. He hopes that the affair will be over in three weeks, and probably Tokar and Sinkat will be relieved at once or not at all. Then General Gordon and Colonel Stewart arrived. We knew the latter well, before, but I could see by his eyes when he bade me farewell, that he had never expected to return from this expedition with Gordon to Khartoum.

It was said that Gordon gave his coat to be given to the poor, also, before he left Cairo.

Miss Wormald was right, for Stewart did not return. He and his companions were massacred near the Fifth Cataract, on the Nile, before the close of the year.

The Diary continues:

Gordon had a most stormy interview with Zubeir at the Agency. Zubeir accused him of having unjustifiably destroyed his relatives, in particular his son, Sulieman, whom Gessi had executed. Gordon angrily replied that he had killed no-one but traitors (when Governor of Equatoria).

Rising to his full height, Zubeir said: 'The charge is true! The blood feud is between us, and I cannot aid you.'

This is probably why none of Zubeir's men would help Valentine in the relief of the garrisons.

Meanwhile it was the greatest moral support to Valentine when his friend Fred Burnaby lightheartedly strode into his camp outside Suakin. Now they could discuss the deplorable situation together. The telegraph line which had never materialised, although it had been promised, the useless old muzzle-loaders, the troops which had never arrived, and those which had arrived, having been forcibly dragged from their homes. Colonel Burnaby was the greatest support and comfort to his friend, through all the difficulties and danger.

Meanwhile a telegram arrived from the Prime Minister which was to prove disastrous both to Valentine Baker and to General Gordon. It was to acquaint him with the Government's definite decision to evacuate the Sudan.

When he first went to the relief of the garrisons, Valentine was under the impression that Her Majesty's Government really meant to administer the Eastern Sudan.

Apart from his own mixed force from Egypt, on his arrival at the port of Suakin he had been able to gather together the Sheikhs of the neighbouring districts, who, at that time, seemed willing and eager to swear allegiance to Great Britain. With their support, he still hoped against hope that armed conflict could have been avoided, and that a mere show of force would have enabled them to quieten the uprising, but, on receipt of the Government's telegram, Valentine felt, although bitterly disappointed, that there was only one honourable course open to him. He at once sent for the principal Sheikh, and explained the position, and asked for his continued support.

The Sheikh insisted upon leaving at once, and declared that all would follow his example. Years later, when lying wounded in England, Valentine explained this to his friends, Douglas Murray, Fred Burnaby and his brother Sam, who were visiting him. Douglas Murray wrote* that Valentine Baker asked the Sheikh, 'Why must he leave?' to which the Sheikh replied: 'We must serve one master. If it is not to be your Government, it must be the Mahdi. Otherwise what will happen to us? Our flocks and herds will be taken away, our wives and children sold into slavery, and we shall all have our throats cut.' Without the help of the friendly Sheikhs, Valentine found himself without any local support at all.

On 11 February, at Berber, just a week after the disastrous battle of El Teb, (See Chapter 17), Gordon, who was on his way to Khartoum,

---

* In *Sir Samuel Baker a Memoir* – published 1895.

received the same telegram, and felt he had to take the same decision. He called the local Chiefs together. On hearing the news the friendly chiefs melted away like snow. They joined the forces of the Mahdi. Gordon felt that the Gladstone administration had been responsible for the loss of many thousands of supporters.

Valentine was to say later: 'I thus lost control of several brave fighting men, all of whom joined the Mahdists, in consequence of our fatuous and suicidal policy.'

* * *

It was because of the lack of support, both from London and also from the local chiefs, that Valentine now decided to move his force to Trinkitat, fifty miles down the coast, and from there attempt to relieve the beleaguered garrison at Tokar.

With his ADC, Major Harvey, Burnaby and Colonel Hay, he embarked in the HMS *Sphinx*, the flagship of Admiral Sir James Hewett, and at length arrived opposite the swampy shore beyond which Trinkitat lay. On the far side of the swamp the troops were organised to build a fort, which would act as 'the advance base' for the march on Tokar. It was very similar to the fortifications which Valentine had built around Constantinople at the close of the Turkish campaign, and 'Fort Baker' was for some years to become a landmark in all future operations. But from the beginning Valentine knew that with only his unwilling troops to support him, it would be almost impossible to defeat the fanatical followers of the Mahdi.

At seven o'clock on the morning of 3 February 1884 the army set out towards Tokar, Colonel Burnaby lightheartedly riding beside Valentine, armed only with a pistol and an umbrella.

As usual, the light cavalry enveloped the line of advance, and the two Krupps guns were well within the large 'British Square' – but as soon as two or three Arabs appeared out of the distance, mounted on camels, the taut nerves of the Egyptians seemed to snap. Fred Burnaby wrote later:

'Now some Arabs, mounted on dromedaries, appeared on our right flank. General Baker ordered one troop of cavalry to drive them in. Instead of one troop riding to the attack, the whole Regiment galloped wildly after this handful of men.'

Panic ensued, Colonel Burnaby rode off in pursuit, but when three Arab horsemen appeared on the brow of the hill, the cavalry broke once

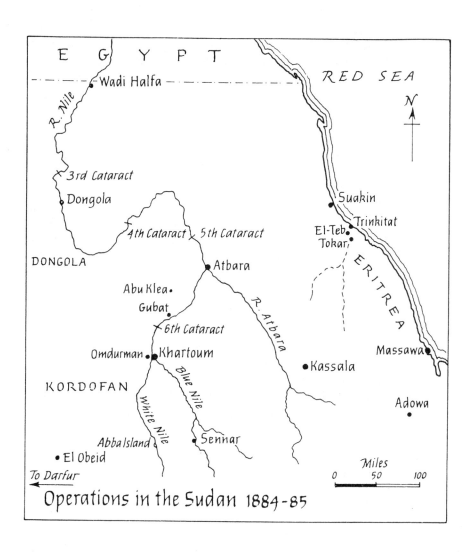

Operations in the Sudan 1884-85

more into a gallop. A moment later a tremendous firing broke out from the troops in the large square. Their fire brought down their own cavalrymen, narrowly missing the General himself as he rode along the lines to attempt to encourage the men.

In the autobiography of Sir Elliot Wood, who also fought with Valentine at El Teb, he wrote how 'In feverish fear they opened fire on Baker and his staff as they fell back to enter the square. They were destroyed by a force a quarter of their strength, for they refused to make even a feeble effort in defence of their lives.'

The disorganisation led to wild confusion. Burnaby continued: 'This completed the confusion. Sticking spurs into their horses, they galloped as fast as they could from the field of battle.' A terrible scene ensued. The square broke up and the flying Egyptians rushed into the two smaller squares, causing the utmost disorder.

> 'The sight,' wrote Burnaby 'was one never to be forgotten, with some four thousand men running pell-mell for their lives, with a few hundred Arabs behind them, spearing everyone within reach. General V. Baker and Colonel Hay with the Arabs between them and the Egyptians, forced a passage through their foes – Egyptians on their knees praying for mercy; English and foreign officers at the guns, surrounded by their assailants, selling their lives dearly . . . English officers doing their best to rally the Egyptians who had been the first to leave the field of battle.'

At last, in the terrible confusion, the swamp which divided them from Trinkitat was crossed. Sir Elliot Wood wrote in his Diary:

> The enemy had cut the line of retreat to Trinkitat and as an all out effort to make any man fight had failed, Baker's staff officer, Fitzroy Hay, finally induced him to leave the field.
> Two Dervishes, with spear and shield closed to bar his way, but he held straight for them. Then, knowing that even if he rode them down, they would get their spears into him or the horse, at the last second he jinked his steed to one side and shot past. As a last chance the men threw their spears, which Hay, who was riding in his wake, saw pass close to his back.

It was only when the situation had become hopeless that Valentine himself crossed the swamp. Burnaby wrote 'He was the last man into Trinkitat.'

The Arabs, tempted by the desire to loot the baggage and equipment thrown down in the retreat, now slackened their pursuit, and the disastrous battle came to an end.

Two thousand, three hundred men lay dead – and ninety officers. Valentine himself sent a bitter telegram to Cairo:

> Our square being only threatened by small force of enemy, certainly less than a thousand strong, Egyptian troops threw down their arms and ran, allowing themselves to be killed without the slightest resistance. More than two thousand killed. All material lost.*

After arriving at Trinkitat, Valentine worked tirelessly saving stores and horses which could otherwise have been lost. But it had been a major disaster. In Cairo, Major Reginald Wingate wrote in his diary:

> *February 6th* Great excitement about the Suakin news. It appears that Baker advanced on Tokar and, when in the act of relieving it, his force, formed in a square, was threatened by a large number of the enemy, and the Egyptians at once flung down their arms, and bolted, carrying the black troops with them. The Europeans and Turks attempted to retreat, and were all killed. Baker made his way back to Trinkitat and thence to Suakin, with 2,000 men, mostly unarmed. Some of the officers were missing, and all the stores, guns, camels etc. have fallen into enemy hands.Great sympathy is felt for Baker, and it is not yet decided what is to be done.
>
> It was said that without his resourcefulness even those men and horses which he saved would have fallen to the enemy.

Fanny Wormald's diary continues from Cairo:

> We heard to-day that Baker Pasha, with 3,500 men, had been defeated by the Mahdi's forces at El Teb on Feb. 4th. A remnant of this force, including Val, with about 1,000 men had escaped to Trinkitat. Val said in his last letter to us, written the night before the battle, that he 'hoped for success, so far as the utterly worthless character of the troops permitted, but that the proclamation of the abandonment of the Sudan had naturally won all the wavering, and even friendly tribes over to the Mahdi.'
>
> Nubar came here three times, and he assured Fanny that, but for Val, every man would have perished.
>
> Sir Samuel and Lady Baker arrived here on Saturday, too late, alas to be able to help.

★ ★ ★

From *The Army Quarterly* 1936.

It must have needed all Valentine Baker's fortitude to face the next three weeks. His gallant attempt to relieve the garrisons of Tokar and Sinkat had completely failed. To a soldier of his experience and reputation any defeat would have been a fearful blow to his pride, but his telegram shows his complete disgust with the troops he was asked to command.

Burnaby described the retreat into Trinkitat:

> A panic prevailed, the Egyptian sailors firing upon the Egyptian soldiers, who attempted to go on board without orders. The remainder of that day and all that night General Baker, who had been the last man into Trinkitat, was at work embarking stores, horses, etc. This, thanks to his extraordinary energy, was eventually accomplished, and the following morning by twelve o'clock what was left of our shattered force was on its way to Suakin.

Fortunately for Valentine there was much to be done, and he threw himself into the welfare of those he had managed to extricate – the men were collected and clothed, the terrified horses groomed and fed, and the stores put on board. Meanwhile the Admiral he so much admired, Admiral Hewett, was in charge of the Port of Suakin.

The news of the disaster reached Cairo on 11 February, and with it the news that Sinkat had fallen. Tewfik Bey had sallied out of the town with 450 men, and all had been massacred, with the exception of five men. Parliament was up in arms, and in spite of protests by the Prime Minister himself it was decided to send British troops to Suakin.

General Stephenson, who was commanding the Army in Egypt, was ordered to send three battalions, and he sent the best, to form the nucleus of the British Expeditionary force. The Black Watch, the Gordon Highlanders, and the 60th Rifles embarked for Suakin. The Cavalry were represented by the 10th* and 19th Hussars, and Major General Sir Gerald Graham VC was given command of the force. On 18 February they set sail from Suez for Suakin, arriving there on 22 February.

Burnaby, still as faithful and true a friend as ever, could so easily have left to rejoin his regiment at home, but preferred to stay to support his friend. He showed himself completely impervious to any anxiety about the future. He lightheartedly said he wished he could have gone up over the battlefield by balloon to inspect the enemy positions, and it was thought that it was due to his advice that a telegram was sent to Sir Evelyn Baring by Admiral Hewett:

---

* The 10th Hussars had been directed from their voyage from India to England (see page 145)

Please ask General to try to find some appointment for Baker in expedition. Intelligence or other. He is terribly down under bad luck, and we all feel for him and like him so much.

The appointment was confirmed at Buckingham Palace. Valentine Baker was appointed as Chief Intelligence Officer to the Army.

In spite of his depression, the appointment must have given him just the encouragement he most needed. After the disaster he was not forgotten. He was, once again, after so many years, although only as an Intelligence Officer, to accompany a British Army in the field.

17

THE BELOVED COLONEL

Meanwhile, the 10th Hussars, Valentine's own regiment, had just embarked from Bombay on their return journey to England after their tour of duty in India. They had been stationed there for ten years, and now, after a very distinguished tour, were delighted to be 'coming home' with their wives and sweethearts on board.

If they had heard news of their Colonel's disgrace so soon after their departure from England, they had not believed it. They were loyal to a man, and they knew that any dishonourable act was entirely foreign to his nature.

Whilst their ship, the *Jumna*, was coaling in Aden, a small steamer drew up alongside and the Regiment was asked to call at the Port for orders.

Conjecture and opinions of all kinds were ventured, and the excitement on board was very great. It was known before leaving India that Egyptian troops had been sent to the Eastern Sudan under Baker Pasha, to relieve the garrisons of Sinkat and Tokar, but it was not thought that the British Government would take part in those operations, so it was with some surprise that the troops found that they were now ordered to take on board camp equipment and disembark at Suakin.

As no-one was allowed on board, because of quarantine regulations, the whole night was passed in taking on board camp equipment and coaling. It was probably the first time that the coaling of one of Her Majesty's ships had been cheerfully performed by a cavalry regiment. They sailed on the following afternoon, the three days in the Red Sea being occupied in preparations for landing, arranging for service kit for the men, and getting the officers' saddlery out of the baggage holds.

The account, in the Regimental History of the 10th Hussars, continues: 'The ladies were busily employed providing useful articles for the campaign.' The men welcomed the call to action, but for their sweethearts and wives the next few weeks must have been a time of great anxiety – the long hoped for journey home, preceded by balls and celebrations in India, by gaiety and Valentine cards when at sea, was suddenly to become a time of military action, but it is on record in the Regimental History that they showed a gallantry quite equal to their men. Their ship was later to become a hospital ship to which all the wounded and sick were taken, and these brave ladies took on all the duties of nurses, despite the anxiety they must have felt for their husbands.

Owing to coral reefs and the weather being rough, it was not until 18 February that the *Jumna* finally sailed into Suakin.

As she came into view, a small group of officers watched her from the deck of HMS *Euryalus*, Admiral Hewett's flagship. Among them, tall and erect in his uniform, and with the star of the Osmanie about his neck, Valentine stood motionless. For he realised that he would soon be able to meet his own regiment, to which he had given his heart, and thirteen of the happiest years of his life.

That afternoon Valentine mounted the gangway of the *Jumna*. The band on deck struck up 'Auld Lang Syne' and he was welcomed by a Guard of Honour. As he stepped forward to shake hands with the Commanding Officer, Colonel Woods, there was a sudden shout, 'Three Cheers for our Colonel!'

The deck was crowded with officers and men, some even up in the rigging, and cheer after cheer now broke out at the sight of their beloved Colonel once again. Helmets were raised and flung into the air. With a full heart he recognised many old comrades – ten years older it is true, and lean and sunburnt from their service in India but all 'cheering themselves hoarse'. It was a very moving moment. The despairing memories of the last few weeks were softened as he clasped Woods' hand.

A military artist, Melton Bird, was to capture the moment for ever, in a sketch made at the time, and which was to appear in England in the *Illustrated London News*. It was drawn in pen and ink (for it was before the use of blocks for printing photographs had been invented). General Baker, dressed in his uniform as General in command of the Egyptian Gendarmerie is seen shaking hands with Colonel Woods, while the Regiment cheered him to the echo.

Valentine at once offered the horses of his three Regiments of Egyptian Gendarmerie to mount the Tenth. Colonel Woods and the

Field Officers landed and were taken by him to inspect the horses, which, because he had chosen and trained them, were in good condition in spite of the ordeal through which they had passed. Three hundred were selected. The saddles, with which Valentine Baker had had to train the Gendarmerie were pitifully old fashioned, mostly having belonged to the French Cavalry, and the bits were of the Mameluke pattern. Admiral Hewett and the officers of the Fleet all helped to remedy their deficiencies. Sailmakers were landed, who set to work to make nose-bags, head and heel ropes. Carbine buckets were improvised by cutting a hole through the shoe cases through which the carbines were passed. In the evening, the horses were ridden for the first time and taken to the wells for water.

The spirits of Valentine and Fred Burnaby now revived. It was glorious to be with trained fighting men once more with all the confidence of their traditions behind them. Burnaby and his friend were now officially Intelligence Officers. Burnaby had armed himself with a shotgun. For some reason the fact that he had used such a weapon, instead, perhaps, of a pistol and umbrella, while on leave from his Regiment, caused a commotion in England on his return.

As Chief Intelligence Officer, Valentine was to act as guide and adviser to General Graham, during the coming engagement.

On 22 February, the 10th had taken part in a Field Day in the presence of the staff and General Baker, and had 'sharpened their swords'. On the 23rd they embarked once more with their horses for Tokar. There they disembarked from rafts on the 25th, as there were no proper harbour installations. On the 28th, orders for readiness to advance were received.

Everything was working in meticulous order. The military advance was organised to perfection. The horses were watered, and at 5 pm the cavalry moved off and reached Fort Baker just after sunset, bivouacking there for the night.

At 8.30 am the next morning, after the men's breakfasts, the force paraded. The infantry moved off into a large square, covered, about a mile in advance, by the first squadron of the 10th Hussars under Major Gough. The remainder of the Cavalry Brigade and mounted infantry were echeloned from the right, the 10th Hussars in first line, the 19th Hussars in second line.

The Infantry Square was led, under the guidance of General Baker himself, to the right of this line, as he hoped to avoid the sad and terrible sight of the line of his recent retreat, where the bodies of the fallen still lay. The ships from the Harbour opened fire to cover the advance, but their shots fell far short of the enemy, so that at a signal from Fort Baker, the firing had to be stopped.

The Infantry Square now moved slowly forward, the cavalry drawing the enemy's fire from the right of his position. Having thus ascertained from which direction the fire was coming, the cavalry returned to its original position and waited for the attack to begin.

The Krupp guns, captured only a few days previously, by the follower of Osman Digna, opened fire upon the Infantry Square, and from the Diary of Sir Elliot Wood we have a description of what followed:

> Baker and I were in the Square together while the enemy were firing case or canister from the guns they had captured at Tokar, which had fallen by this time. The range was long for the class of shot, so the balls were hitting the sand short of the men and were ricochetting over their heads. We were discussing the situation when Baker clapped his hand to his face, at the same time twitching his bridle, so that his horse spun right round, yet without shifting him in the saddle. I thought a pebble had hit him, as he quietly rode to the ambulance and in five minutes returned to me with his face strapped up. The Cavalry Brigade-Major had ridden into the Square to ask in which direction the main body of the enemy were retiring. But just after we told him, we saw the enemy turned back, full of fight. I asked Baker who seemed heedless of his wound 'If the Cavalry might not be advised?' – 'Certainly,' he replied, 'If anyone can get to them' – so out I galloped. That night Baker was feverish, and Sir Gerald sent him back to HMS *Sphinx* at Trinkitat. The Naval surgeon found 2 oz iron ball lodged in his cheek, having broken into the palate. The marvel was that he was not knocked off his horse. The wound caused much trouble for years.

Meanwhile Burnaby was also wounded in the upper arm by flying shrapnel, and his horse was shot under him. Both he and Valentine seemed quite oblivious of their wounds during the battle which followed.

With military precision the Square advanced, but the Arabs rushed with fanatical bravery towards it, and many hundreds were killed. The 10th and 19th Hussars took a few prisoners, but, according to the official records:

> The Cavalry Brigade now found large numbers of the enemy among the bush, and the two Regiments charged again and again, eventually dispersing them. The ground in many places was covered with high mimosa bush, the thorns of which the horses avoided, and, as this caused gaps in the ranks,

opportunities were given to the active enemy of rushing out from their hiding-places and of hamstringing the horses and stabbing their riders.

Major Slade, of the 10th Hussars, while wheeling his Squadron from the flank, was attacked by several Arabs on all sides and killed. Lieutenant Probyn was also killed, but 'the appearance of his sword afterwards showed that the enemy had paid dearly for their success.' 'Sergeant Cox, too, as fine a soldier as ever served in the Regiment, who had often carried off the regimental prize for swordsmanship, thinking that he saw a good opportunity, left the flank of his squadron and charged a group of savages, but being overpowered by numbers, lost his life . . . The infantry continued to advance through the enemy's position round the wells, keeping up a tremendous fire, and marched over the rifle pits and entrenchments.'

At this moment, Fred Burnaby, on foot, was the first man to reach the defences. He leapt on to the parapet only to be surrounded by Arabs and their spears. He fired off both barrels of his shotgun and, unable to re-load, began to fight with only the butt of his gun. A huge Highlander dashed to his defence, and with a bayonet saved his life.

Soon the infantry, advancing stolidly over the defences, put the Arabs to flight and the retreat soon became nothing less than a rout. Valentine and Burnaby realised that victory had at last been achieved.

Before the bivouac was formed, Baker Pasha, although he must have been in great pain from his wound, with a bullet still in his face below the eye, rode along the 10th's lines to enquire after his old regiment and to congratulate it upon the day. Sir William Hewett also visited the Regiment, and, returning to his flagship, signalled the ladies on board the *Jumna* the condition of the wounded and also the names of those who had lost their lives in action.

Until he had ridden down the lines of his old regiment Valentine had refused to acknowledge that he had been wounded. He wanted to show the men of the 10th Hussars how proud he was to have been with them that day.

After the great victory, although the Regiment was to stay another month in the Sudan, and to re-capture almost all the arms and ammunition which had been taken in the first battle, Valentine was not with them, as he had been forced to return to Egypt for treatment of his wound. Fanny Wormald again takes up the account. She wrote:–

Val was examined the next day. The doctor found splinters of bone to remove, and this large bullet which had gone through his cheek-bone as if it had been shot through a door. It had to be sawn out, and poor Val sat in an armchair, being cut about for ¾ of an hour, without chloroform and without flinching or moving a muscle, except that once he fainted with the agony. He told Fanny it was a very bad ten minutes! Colonel Hay said he had pulled up wonderfully the last five days. For the first three days he bled a great deal in his mouth, then lost his voice, partly with his throat being affected, and partly from weakness. He has of course grown much thinner, but he could not have got on better, they say. His health must have been perfect. He is patience itself and never even seems weary of his long time in bed, and it is now more than two weeks since he was hit.

He heard in Suez that he was restored to the English Army and it has made him so happy – I do hope it may be true, for it would be a most bitter disappointment if it were not.

Tuesday – Alas! There was a telegram today to say no truth I fear in report. We have not ventured to tell Val. . . . Dear Mrs. Hopkinson, you must forgive more.

Yours affectionately,
Fanny Wormald.

She adds, 'Mione going on well, but still very feeble and needing care.'*

The telegram countermanding the good news was only too accurate. On 11 March, less than a fortnight after the victory, Sir Henry Ponsonby had written to the Queen.

Windsor Castle.
March 11th 1884.

To Her Gracious Majesty,

General Sir Henry Ponsonby humbly begs leave to report that the Duke of Cambridge went over the whole of the Baker case, and the account of his recent services, urging that, as he had been severely punished, he might now be pardoned and restored nominally as a retired officer.

Sir Henry Ponsonby asked His Royal Highness if he, or the Secretary of State intended to advise the Queen to this effect.

He said he could not well do so himself (as Commander-in-Chief) but asked if your Majesty would initiate the suggestion.

Sir Henry Ponsonby said that it was impossible and that he knew your Majesty was opposed to such a proposal.

The Duke replied that he was not aware of this. He imagined that Mr. Gladstone only was the objector to Baker's restoration.

Your humble and respectful servant, Ma'am,
Sir Henry Ponsonby.

This letter is in the possession of Mrs. Valentine Baker.

A further letter followed to the Duke of Cambridge.

March 28th 1884.

Sir,

I thought it right to send General Stephenson's letter to the Queen last night, as it is so well and moderately expressed, and I thought it possible that Her Majesty might have spoken to Lord Hartington upon it.

I find this morning that Her Majesty did not mention the subject, but she told me that she could not consent to Baker Pasha's restoration to the English Army.

I have the honour to be, Sir, Your Royal Highness,
Your obedient and humble servant,
Henry Ponsonby.

It was a mark of great appreciation for General Stephenson to have written to the Duke of Cambridge concerning Valentine and equally remarkable that the Duke of Cambridge had written himself to the Queen. But their thoughtful recommendations were of no avail. The Queen still did not feel that she could restore him to the British Army.

Meanwhile, as news of the Sudan came through to the people in England, feelings were running high. Reports of the battle were appearing in all the newspapers, and there were many tales of heroism on the parts of both officers and men. One of the bravest was Trooper Hayes of the 10th Hussars, who was a skilled pugilist.

Determined to rescue a wounded comrade, he had dismounted and attacked a number of Arabs, knocking them down with his fists, before re-mounting with the friend he had rescued in front of his saddle. Trooper Hayes was afterwards thanked by General Graham himself for his courage and a year later he received the Distinguished Service Medal, presented by the Queen herself. A fortnight after the battle an amazing poem appeared in *Punch*, not only praising Trooper Hayes, but also paying a splendid tribute to Valentine Baker. Written in typically sentimental Victorian verse, it still carries an impassioned appeal for Valentine's restoration to the Army, an appeal which must have reflected not only the deep devotion of the 10th Hussars to their old Colonel, but the feelings of the whole country.

It ran:–

A Tale of the Tenth Hussars
When the sand of the lonely desert had covered the plains of strife
When the English fought for the rescue, and the Arab stood for his life,

When the crash of the battle is over, and healed are our wounds and scars,
There will live in our Island Story, a tale of the 10th Hussars.
They had charged in the grand old fashion, with furious shout and swoop
With a 'Follow me, lads' from the Colonel, and an answering roar from the
troop;
On the Staff as the troopers passed it, in glorious pride and pluck,
They heard, and they never forgot it, one following shout, 'Good luck!'
Wounded and worn he sat there, in silence of pride and pain,
The man who had led them often, but was never to lead again!
Think of the secret anguish – think of the dull remorse,
To see the Hussars sweep past him, unled by the old white horse.

An alien, not a stranger, with heart of a comrade still,
He had borne his sorrow bravely, as a soldier must and will;
And when the battle was over, in deepening gloom and shade,
He followed the Staff in silence and rode to the grand parade;

For the Tenth had another hero, all ripe for the General's praise,
Who was called to the front that evening, by the name of Trooper Hayes.
He had slashed his way to a fortune, when scattered, unhorsed, alone
And in saving the life of a comrade, he managed to guard his own.

The General spoke out bravely, as ever a soldier can,
'The Army's proud of your valour, the Regiment's proud of its man.'

Then across the lonely desert, at the close of the General's praise,
Came a cheer, then a quick short tremble, on the lips of Trooper Hayes.
'Speak out,' said the kindly Colonel, 'if you've anything, lad, to say,
Your Queen and your dear old country shall hear what you've done today.'

But the trooper gnawed his chin-strap, then sheepishly hung his head.
'Speak out, old chap' said his comrades. With an effort at last he said:
'I came to the front with my pals here, the boys and the brave old tars,
I've fought for my Queen and country, and rode with the 10th Hussars;
I'm proud of the fine old regiment –' Then the Colonel shook his hand,
'So I'll ask one single favour from my Queen and my native land.
There sits by your side on the Staff, Sir, a man we are proud to own,
He was struck down first in the battle, but never was heard to groan,
If I've done ought to deserve it..' Then the General smiled, 'of course',
'Give back to the Tenth their Colonel, the man on the old white horse.

If ever a man bore up, Sir, as a soldier should with pluck
And fought with a savage sorrow, the Demon of cursed ill-luck
That man he sits before you! Give us back with his wounds and scars

The man who has sorely suffered, and is loved by the Tenth Hussars.'

Then a cheer went up from his comrades, and echoed across the sand,
And was borne on wings of mercy to the hearts of his native land,
Where the Queen on her throne will hear it, and the Colonel Prince will praise
The words of a simple soldier, just uttered by Trooper Hayes.

Let the moralists stoop to mercy, that balm of all souls that live;
For better than all forgetting,
Is the wonderful word 'Forgive'.

But in spite of these verses being re-printed in almost every paper in the country, the Queen did not find it in her heart to forgive, until it was too late.

★   ★   ★

At the beginning of May it was thought that Valentine's wound needed more specialised attention, and he returned to London with his family. Advance news of his arrival had spread, and quite a crowd gathered at Charing Cross Station to meet him, and to cheer him on his arrival.

One man slapped him on the back, and said: 'You are a fine fellow, General, and we are proud of you!'

His niece Helen, with her mother, was among those who met him. She said:

> His face was still bandaged when he arrived. A stream of well-wishers and friends called at his hotel, and she [her mother] was allowed to see him herself for only a moment and he was very tired. . . . *The Times* is full of Uncle Val's defeat, but he is being praised on all sides, and they say that no-one but Uncle Val would have undertaken an expedition with so forlorn a hope . . .

In July, Valentine was sufficiently recovered to be asked by his sister to this same niece's wedding. He wrote:

> Marlborough Club,
> Pall Mall SW
> July 24th 1884

My dearest Annie,

I have delayed answering your letter in the hope that I might be able to accept your kind invitation to Ruth's wedding, but I find we cannot possibly manage it. All our very best wishes for her happiness.

I am getting on steadily, but the doctors will not let me go back until the end of September.

'Mione is also doing well, but I shall be very glad to get her away from London. When are you likely to be in Town? We leave on Saturday for Southsea.

Love to all, and Ever dearest Annie,

Your affectionate brother,

V. Baker.*

The interest of this letter is that it not only shows how long it took Valentine to recover from his severe wound, but also, as he wrote on the headed writing paper of the Marlborough Club, it is again proof of the loyalty of the Prince of Wales, for Valentine was to remain a member of the most exclusive Club in London all his life.

It was during the summer, also, that the Prince and Princess of Wales reviewed the troops who had returned from the recent battle on the banks of the Red Sea. It was a brilliant event, and General Valentine Baker, as Intelligence Officer, and Colonel Burnaby, were present. Valentine was, as usual, mounted on a grey long-tailed Arab, and it was a proud moment for him as he watched the 10th Hussars marching past the Prince of Wales.

---

* This letter is in the possession of the Baker family.

18

GORDON AND KHARTOUM

Meanwhile, in spite of the second battle of El Teb, which had momentarily checked the followers of Osman Digna, the sinister power of the mysterious Mahdi was growing throughout the Sudan. The native Chiefs, assured now of the British Government's intention to withdraw their forces, flocked to his banner.

General Gordon had, at first, received an enthusiastic welcome on the arrival at Khartoum on 18 January. To the garrison it had seemed that they were not forgotten, and for a few weeks things seemed to improve. Gordon telegraphed to Sam Baker on hearing the news from Suakin. The telegram ran:–

Khartoum,
February 26th 1884

By your letter, 26th January, you are in Cairo. Hope all well. Sorry Suakin business. Tell your brother Heads or Tails up here! But will trust –

Gordon

Another telegram dated 29 February ran:–

Thanks, we are all right up here for the present . . . You and Lady Baker would enjoy the excitement. It is a question of weeks but hope to pull through.

One last telegram reached Sir Samuel, before the tribes north of Khartoum rose, and the telegraph line was cut, thus isolating Gordon at Khartoum.

Gordon wrote:

> I have received a meagre telegram from Baring to the effect that it is not
> intended to send British troops to open the road to Berber, but that nego-
> tiations are going on with Arabs for opening the road. You will be able to
> judge of the value of such negotiations with the Arabs and also of the time
> any such arrangements would last after the withdrawal of the British from
> Suakin.

He continued:

> I am in this position – we have provisions for five months – are hemmed in
> by some 5,000 determined men and some 2,000 rag-tag Arabs. As you
> know, our position will be much strengthened when the Nile rises. Sennar,
> Kassala, Dongola and Berber are quite safe for the present.

Gordon suggested that Sir Samuel might launch an appeal to million-
aires in America and England, so that an army could be raised to open
the road to Berber, and suggested that Zubeir might command it. His
telegram concluded:

> I feel sure that if it was known the way the townspeople and troops have
> held to me in such difficult circumstances and the way my lot is involved
> with theirs, I should be justified in making this appeal. I should be mean,
> indeed, if I neglected any steps that would occur to me for the security of
> their safety.

The appeal was actually made, and, no doubt, Sam was in large part
responsible, but owing to the Government's attitude, Gordon's advice
was not acted upon.

Meanwhile, the telegraph went dead and Khartoum was isolated. Gradually news filtered through to Cairo and London and it became clear
that somehow Gordon must be rescued.

But even now the Government were slow to realise the gravity of the
situation, and slow to take any military action. Had Valentine Baker
been commanding the Army in Egypt, one cannot help wondering if the
tragic history of that year might have been different. One cannot help
wondering too if Gordon would never have been sacrificed to the
hesitant policy of the Government and whether, under Valentine's more
daring leadership and with the advice of his brother Sir Samuel, who
knew the Sudan so well, the Relief Expedition, when it finally left
Egypt, would not have arrived in time. But Valentine was recovering

from his wound in London and was quite powerless to influence the situation.

His friend, Fred Burnaby, however, was far from silent. Speaking in Birmingham he described the two battles in which he had just fought. He explained that General Valentine Baker's original intentions were to relieve Tokar and Sinkat, with the help of the friendly native Chiefs, if possible without bloodshed, but that the announcement by Gladstone of the British withdrawal from the Sudan had led to the complete loss of support from the Chiefs and also led to the two fearful battles. He implored the Government to send help to Gordon:

> I feel there is not one man, not one woman, not one child in England,' he said, 'who, if the case were put straightforwardly before them, would not at once say 'Spare no money, but rescue General Gordon'.

All summer the feelings in England were rising to fever pitch. Even so, the Relief Expedition under General Wolseley seemed to take far too long to arrange. In reply to a letter from Sam, recommending suitable boats for navigating the river Nile, Sir Garnet Wolseley wrote:

> *War Office,*
> *23rd August 1884*
>
> My dear Sir Samuel,
>   Many thanks for your kind and very flattering letter of yesterday. I have also read your interesting letter which is published in *The Times*. I think if you had seen the rivers ascended and descended during the Red River Expedition you would admit that the same class of boats they used could be taken anywhere on the Nile which is a mild affair when compared with the North American rivers along which the whole trade of the Hudson Bay and North West companies has been conveyed in boats for the last century. The Nile Boats can only be used successfully above Barcal when the river is full, or tolerably full, whereas our row boats can go anywhere no matter how low it may be; indeed the lower it is, the better for a boat expedition, and we have delayed so long in making preparations for the despatch of an Expedition that should we be forced to send in a force South of Wadi-Halfa – for which no orders have yet been issued, it would be impossible to reach Khartoum by water at all this coming winter except in boats of the description we are using.

And so Sam, who knew the Nile so well, was not consulted about the most suitable boats. He must have been appalled at the irrelevance of comparing the expedition to the Red River in Canada. At this time he was also to receive a letter from the Duke of Somerset:

> Dear Sir Samuel,
> The public opinion is beginning to be ashamed of leaving Khartoum to the rebels. The French offering to send troops must stimulate our Ministries – I have read your paper on the Sudan. It helps to give people a notice of what we are doing in abandoning the Sudan.
> Yours, Somerset.

In spite of all Sam's efforts, in spite of public consternation and great anxiety shown by the Queen herself, it was not until 16 September that Lord Wolseley arrived in Cairo, and it was not until 8 October, five months after communications had been interrupted, that permission to attempt to reach Khartoum was granted to the Expeditionary Force. There were six cataracts to be negotiated before reaching Khartoum, and there were six steamers in the expedition besides the unfortunate 'Whaler Boats' so unwisely insisted upon by Lord Wolseley. Sir Ronald Wingate was to write later:

> This was an unfortunate error, as the boats, laden with supplies, had to be unloaded during the stages of portage, and then reladen, and the pace of the expedition in the initial stages was the pace of the slowest boat – about a mile a day. Later, native boats were used which were much more suitable.*

Meanwhile all through the long hot summer, letters continued to arrive in Cairo and in London from General Gordon. It was easier for letters to leave Khartoum than for letters to reach him, for many were glad to leave the city, while few were willing or able to slip through the Mahdi's lines with news. Gordon felt more and more isolated as he stood on the roof of the Palace, looking out towards the curve of the river Nile from which he hoped help would come.

It was Captain Kitchener who managed to set up an advance post at Debba, from which he hoped to keep up communications with Khartoum. He was tireless in helping to get messages and letters through, and even disguised himself as a bedouin in order to slip through the enemy lines with vital and important news.

One bundle of letters, wrapped in an old English newspaper, and

---

* From *The Life of Sir Reginald Wingate*

delivered by Kitchener's runners, was almost thrown away in the Palace courtyard before Gordon himself rescued it. It contained a letter from Sam. On the envelope was written *'Communications avec le Soudan Interrompées'*. Gordon wrote in his Diary 'I should think the communications were *interrompées!*' Sam had written: 'The man whom I have placed my hopes upon, Major Kitchener, RE is one of the *very superior* British Officers, with a cool and good head and a hard constitution combined with untiring energy.'

It was a prophetic statement. In one of his last letters dated 5 November 1884, Gordon wrote to Sam:

Dear Sir Samuel,
Your kind letter dated June 1st reached me yesterday. I am glad your brother [Valentine] is well again, also to hear of Lady Baker and your daughters.

What a rage Hills must be in with me. Remember the expedition comes up 'For the Relief of Garrisons' which I failed to accomplish. It does not come up for *me*! I am glad Mr. Barnes has been to see you at your pretty house (Sam was back in England in June). Are you coming out again to Cairo this year? I shall not come to England again. I cannot stand it, but shall go to Brussels. I had a letter dated June 1st from Stanley in the Congo . . .

He then mentions the boat which had so disastrously been captured by the Mahdi's forces on its way to Berber:

On 10th September, at full Nile, Stewart, Power and Herbin (the French Consul) left here in a small ironclad with good force and a gun on her to go down to Dongola. Kitchener, October 4th, says she was captured and all are killed.

It is terrible! How it happened I cannot make out; either she was captured by treachery or struck a rock, and I had put wooden buffers on her to prevent that. If it is true, and I fear that it is, for our steamers escorted her as far as Berber, then the Journal of events, from 1st Mar 1884 to September 10th is lost, it was a large volume full of details; the general opinion here was that it was a certainty she would get down safe.

I have placed 5 steamers at Mattema to wait arrival of the force "to relieve Garrisons". Kindest regards to yourself and the Miss Bakers and with many thanks for all you have done –
Your sincerely C.E. Gordon

Finally, one last letter arrived:

My dear Sir Samuel,
Thank you for your kind letter of July 17th. We are about to be hemmed in
here . . . all roads cut off and we must eventually fall, and with Khartoum
fall all the other places . . . I have no time for more and doubt if you will
get this, for we may expect the roads cut to-day or tomorrow. If the Nile
were high it would be easier.
    Believe me, with kindest regards to Lady Baker yourself and your family,
            Yours sincerely, C.E. Gordon

★ ★ ★

Meanwhile, at home, Burnaby was determined to join in the Relief
Expedition. He had been invited to join by General Wolseley himself in
a letter ending, 'Hoping we may meet on the Banks of the Nile.' But he
was afraid that he would not be granted leave, especially after the commotion in London when he had fought beside Valentine at Trinkitat
'with a shotgun'. However, he managed to gain five months' leave from
his regiment without specifically mentioning his intentions.

He had already recommended two of his young officers, Lord Arthur
Somerset, and Lord Binney for the 'Camel Corps' (of four regiments)
which had been selected from volunteers as an ancillary to the main
army, and which had sailed from Portsmouth on 26 September.
Burnaby was soon to follow, but in a private capacity.

Before leaving London, he asked Valentine to be guardian to his only
son, then aged four years old. He seemed to have a premonition of
disaster, and a fatalistic feeling that he might not return. On 4
December he finally joined Lord Wolseley at Wadi Halfa, where he was
immediately given the position of Inspecting Staff Officer.

By December, it was already almost impossible to reach Khartoum in
time to rescue Gordon and relieve the garrisons.

On 31 December Gordon sent a last messenger through the Mahdi
lines:

We are besieged on all three sides. Fighting goes on day and night. Our
troops are suffering through want of provisions. The food we have is little,
some grain and biscuits. We want you to come quickly. You should come
by Mehetma and Berber.

This message had been learnt by heart, by the messenger – Gordon would not risk sending a letter.

There was not a moment to lose: Fred Burnaby was, to his delight, put in charge of a grain caravan at Korti with orders to overtake the Camel Corps, an advance party of which was marching across the desert to meet Gordon's steamers at Mehetma, in advance of the main column under Lord Wolseley.

They met near a deep ravine at Abu Klea and bivouacked there for the night, having watered their camels and horses. Early next morning, despite the caution of General Stewart, who had commanded the cavalry at the Second Battle of El Teb, nothing could prevent the fanatical followers of the Mahdi from sweeping down on the British Square which had been formed before the walls of Abu Klea.

Showing a disregard of all danger, as usual, Burnaby encouraged his men to the last, helping them to regain their positions within the Square, but making no effort to join them. A 'furious chief' charged him on horseback, but a bullet soon flung him to the ground. In a moment, however, one of the tribesmen had speared Burnaby in the throat. It was a fatal wound, and, supported by Lord Binney, he lay dying on the field of battle.

After the engagement, the news spread like wildfire. It seemed unthinkable that the brave and gallant 'Burnaby of the Blues' could have so suddenly lost his life. Many strong men were in tears. A Union Jack was placed over his body and he was buried under a stone cairn a few yards from where he fell.

Back in Cairo, Valentine heard the news with a very heavy heart. His greatest friend, who had fought beside him so bravely in Turkey and on the border of the Red Sea – and in whom he could always confide – had been taken from him.

Only a few days later, the terrible news came through, that the Expeditionary Force had arrived too late to save General Gordon. On 28 January, when the ships finally sailed, under heavy fire, towards Khartoum, it was seen that the Union Jack was no longer flying from the roof of the Palace, and it soon became clear that Khartoum had fallen.

Reginald Wingate, in Cairo, on hearing the news wrote in his Diary:

> The two steamers, with Sir C. Wilson, Gascoigne, Wortley and 20 NCOs and men of the Royal Sussex Regiment left Gubat for Khartoum on 24th: they had great difficulty in navigating the river owing to its shallow state, and were constantly fired at from the banks. On rounding the SE corner of Tuti Island, a heavy fire was poured upon them from 5 points and from

Khartoum itself, which they could see plainly and which appeared to be wrecked – the Government House had no flag flying and all seemed to point to the town being in the hands of the enemy.

The Relief expedition had arrived just two days too late. Khartoum had been taken on 26 January, and, standing alone on the steps of the old Palace, Gordon had been murdered.

At Sandford Orleigh Sam raged against the Government's slow and dilatory policy. In speaking of the Prime Minister, afterwards known as the Grand Old Man, he would reverse the initials of this sobriquet and for G.O.M. would write M.O.G. (Murderer of Gordon) – so bitterly did he feel.

In Cairo, Valentine had had to face another great personal sorrow. His beloved elder daughter, Hermione, had grown worse, and, before the end of January her young life had quietly slipped away.

Hermione was much loved in Cairo, and on 23 January 1885 her funeral was described in the paper:

> The funeral took place this afternoon, and was attended by the whole of the English colony, by many foreigners, and by all the Ministries and principal officers of state. The coffin was covered by a Union Jack, and was hidden by masses of white flowers. The funeral car was drawn by troopers of the 19th Hussars, and was preceded by an Escort of Gendarmerie. More than a hundred carriages followed in procession.

Hermione was only eighteen. Her early death had brought tragedy to her romance with Kitchener. The story is told in the words of Agatha Twining, her cousin:

> There is no doubt that Lord Kitchener was engaged to Hermione, the eldest daughter of Valentine Baker Pasha. Her death was a great tragedy in Lord Kitchener's life and he never thought of marrying again. He always wore under his shirt a gold locket containing a beautiful miniature of Hermione. This secret was told to me by Hermione's sister, Sybil. . . .
> Before sailing for Russia (in HMS *Hampshire* in which he perished during the Great War) Lord Kitchener sent this precious locket to my eldest sister, Lady Wood. When it was known that Lord Kitchener was dead, my brother-in-law, Major General Sir Elliot Wood, insisted on the locket being returned to the Baker family [by whom it is still held].

To everyone's despair, Hermione's mother, Fanny, who had been so loyal to Valentine through all the difficulties and dangers, and had nursed him so devotedly when he was wounded, herself died in Egypt only a month later. Valentine was left with only his little daughter of fourteen, Sybil, to care for and protect during the next two sad years.

19

A GALLANT SOLDIER LAID TO REST

Perhaps it was the silent devotion to duty which Valentine Baker was to show in the next two years – or perhaps it was sympathy in his sorrow, which prompted the Queen to re-consider her decision about his restoration in the Spring of 1887.

During that time, Egypt had remained peaceful, under the wise guidance of Sir Evelyn Baring, now Lord Cromer. The Relief Expedition, which had set out with so much confidence in September 1884, was to fall back on the Egyptian border and be replaced by a defensive frontier force, for it was still believed during that year that the Mahdi would advance on Egypt.

However, the Mahdi, far away in Omdurman, showed no sign, after the fall of Khartoum, of wanting to extend his conquests any further. It was said that after the death of General Gordon he retreated to his own house across the river at Omdurman and, while still appearing before his devoted followers every evening in his patched 'jibbeh' at the time of the 'Call to Prayer', he never again led his army into battle. Already his power had extended as far as Wadi Halfa to the North, and although the British still had a tentative hold at Suakin, Valentine's headquarters in the First Battle of El-Teb, the rest of the Red Sea Coast had fallen into the hands of Osman Digna. It was only through the vigilance of Major Reginald Wingate, now in charge of Army Intelligence in Egypt, that information was gained – usually from captured documents or from escaped prisoners. Otherwise all reliable communication with Khartoum and the Sudan had ceased.

General Stephenson, in command of the new Egyptian Army, with Kitchener and Wingate, worked very closely with General Baker Pasha and the police. Indeed, Sir Evelyn Baring was to say that he met Valentine almost every day.

From the tattered force who had retreated from Suakin, Valentine had now created one of the most reliable and smartest bodies of men, and as he rode through the streets of Cairo on his favourite white charger, to inspect them, he became once more a well-known and much respected figure who, after the turmoil of the last few years, had brought orderliness and a sense of security to the lives of the people. Both Egyptians and Europeans admired him for his courage and his devotion to duty.

At home, his beloved regiment had received yet another honour. For in June, 1886 Prince Albert Victor, the Prince of Wales' eldest son, joined the 10th Hussars. The members of Wolseley's Camel Corps also returned that summer to Cairo. Captain and Adjutant, the Earl of Airlie, who had been wounded with Burnaby at Abu Klea, rejoined the 10th at Aldershot. He had been twice mentioned in Despatches, and promoted to Brigade Major of the Camel Corps. But there was sadness over those who were not to return, and who had fallen in battle.

In the late April of 1887, the Queen's Jubilee year, Valentine and his pretty young daughter, Sybil, came home for a well-earned six months holiday in England. They were to stay with Sam and Florence in Devonshire, where they would always be welcome. For Sam had made Sandford Orleigh a very happy family home. The wide terrace, facing south, looked over lawns and gardens stretching down towards the river Teign, and, in the peaceful atmosphere, a vista of cypresses led down to a thatched 'Palaver House', built in the style of Central Africa, which was a source of great pride and amusement to him.

The library, hall and staircase were hung with trophies, heads of rhinoceros and hippopotami – even a crocodile's head with a bead necklace hanging fearfully from its jaws – adorned the walls, and tiger skins and tusks of African elephants hung in the Billiard room. In spite of this, the atmosphere was one of relaxation and calm, although the house was often full of visitors.

That summer particularly, Valentine was to feel the restfulness of the long June days in the country, contrasting so vividly with the hot and arid climate of an Egyptian summer. His anxiety about his daughter's happiness was also relieved, for she was cared for and spoilt by her kind Aunt Florence, and her two older cousins.

It was a very happy time, and perhaps also, as it was the year in which the Queen was to celebrate her Jubilee, Valentine might have had some faint hope that the Queen might relent. But he heard nothing.

Meanwhile, a wave of devotion and loyalty swept over the country. In London all the preparations for the Jubilee were put into the capable hands of the Prince of Wales.

The Queen was so grateful. She wrote that if the Prince had not been so very kind and helpful she could not have managed. She was happy that she now felt closer to her eldest son than ever before, and in her gratitude she felt that perhaps she might re-consider the case of his friend, General Valentine Baker, which had always been a barrier between them. Especially this was so now. After the last few years, for while others had been decorated for their part in the battles of El Teb and Abu Klea, he had received no mark of appreciation and yet he had never once complained. One wonders if perhaps new evidence had also at last come to light, for early in June, a rather enigmatic letter was sent from Windsor Castle to Knollys, the Prince's Private Secretary, saying that Lord Ponsonby had seen the Duke of Cambridge and Lord Horsfall, and that they had agreed that it would be undesirable that any measure of inquiry should be instituted by the Queen 'as to Baker Pasha' adding, it would certainly be published, and could occasion a 'good deal of surprise'.

Could it have been that one of the three friends mentioned by Sam so many years before, at the time of the trial, had come forward to tell the Prince of Wales or the Queen of Valentine's innocence? Or had Miss Dickinson herself taken the 'noble course' suggested by Sam twelve years before, and decided, after searching her conscience, to write privately to the Prince of Wales?

Certainly on 15 June only five days before Jubilee Day the Queen was writing to her eldest son:

Windsor Castle
June 15th 1887

To HRH the Prince of Wales.

Dearest Bertie,
As regards General Baker, after consulting some important people in whose judgement I can rely, I now propose that his re-instatement in the Army might take place – by-and-by, but not on account of my Jubilee . . .

The Prince of Wales wrote to his mother the next day:

From HRH The Prince of Wales to Her Majesty the Queen.
My dearest Mamma,
I quite understand your decision about General Baker and if he can be

restored to his original rank as a General next month, before he returns to Egypt, it will be most satisfactory.

Your devoted and affectionate son,

Bertie.

As so often happened, Queen Victoria was able to relent when she felt it was right to do so, and during that year, in all the preparations for her Jubilee, she still remembered the appeals of the Prince of Wales and his loyalty to his friend. Only five days before the celebration, she had written to him, hoping to wipe out at last the injustice which the Prince felt had followed Valentine's years of devoted service.

Delays, however, occurred. The decision had to go before the Military authorities, and it was not till later in the year, that the news could be announced. Meanwhile Valentine heard nothing.

He must have read with pride of the honour done to his Regiment. The Tenth Hussars, resplendent in their dress uniforms and with the new scarlet shabracque and shell bridle for the horses, breastplate and crupper approved by Her Majesty [these appointments had fallen into disuse after the return of the Regiment from the Crimea but were re-instated on 23 May 1884], marched to London. They proceeded by way of Hampton Court to Olympia. There the horses were fed and watered, before being ridden in formation to Buckingham Palace. They lined the streets from the Palace, up Constitution Hill, along Piccadilly to its junction with St James' Street, protecting the route by which Queen Victoria, who insisted on wearing a 'bonnet' and not her crown, passed by in her splendid carriage on her way to Westminster Abbey.

It was a magnificent day.

On 9 July this was followed by a Jubilee Review of the whole Army, 48,000 troops being present. All branches of the Cavalry were repre-sented, and Valentine's old comrade Lord Valentia was commanding the Oxford Yeomanry. The Prince of Wales, as a Field Marshal, marched at the head of the 10th Hussars past the Queen and Prince Albert Victor commanded the right troop of the leading Squadron.

Just a month later, after the restful summer, Valentine was due to return once more to Egypt, still not knowing of the forgiveness of his Queen.

With a heavy heart he travelled to Cairo in July. His daughter, Sybil, who was now seventeen, was to follow, travelling with Ethel and Agatha, Sam's two daughters, who were to stay a short time with their cousin in Egypt before continuing their journey to Newa Ralia in Ceylon. But their journey was delayed and it was not until 9

168

November that they arrived at Port Said. From the very first it was obvious that their uncle was not at all well. The Doctor eventually allowed them to go aboard the *diahbeah*, but Valentine was still feverish, and depressed, although determined to carry out his planned inspection of members of the Gendarmerie who were stationed along the Sweet Water Canal.

The time for the inspection came and the *diahbeah* sailed slowly from her moorings, with his daughter and two cousins on board. A few days later, on the 16th, Valentine struggled up on deck to watch the river Nile, as it slid quietly by, and looked beyond at the flat, sandy, sun-baked shore for the last time.

It was sad to be so far from home. In spite of all his efforts, he still felt exiled. He felt he had been denied the opportunity to serve his Country as he once would have wished. He stood there until sunset, when the sky glowed with brief golden glory, and when night fell, with the suddenness of the East, he quietly returned to his cabin where Sybil came to kiss him goodnight.

Early in the morning, his nieces found him suffering from pains in his shoulders and chest. They gave him laudanum but there was really nothing they could do. In her diary, 'Ettie' wrote, '. . . a little later, he looked as if he was asleep'. But they knew that that brave and gallant life had slipped away.

★   ★   ★

The news was quickly sent to Cairo and the Duke of Cambridge, aware of the Queen's decision, ordered a funeral with full military honours. A special train was sent to bring his mortal remains back to Cairo. In a letter, describing the scene, his sister wrote: 'The Account of the Grief of People in Cairo is very touching.' Ethel wrote: 'All dear Uncle Val's friends seem as if they had lost a father or brother in him.'

When the party reached Cairo at midnight on 17 November, Lord Dunmore, who was at the station 'to meet his friend' as he said, went on to General Stephenson's house a few minutes before the coffin arrived, and found the old General, who was himself only just recovering from fever, standing bare-headed awaiting the sad arrival. His Aide-de-Camp entreated him to go in and to cover his head, knowing what a trial it would be to him, but in vain. He said: 'I shall stand here as I am, though I die for it, to receive my old friend Valentine Baker, the bravest soldier England has ever had.'

The report in *The Times* ran thus:

Death of Baker Pasha

(from our Correspondent) *Cairo – Thursday*

The sad news was received at Cairo to-day at one o'clock of the sudden death of Baker Pasha, better known as Colonel Valentine Baker, which took place on board his steam launch at Tel-el-Kebir. The news was immediately telegraphed to the Duke of Cambridge and a special train was despatched from Cairo with Coles Pasha, Captain and Mrs. Fortescue and Dr Sandwich, to bring back the mortal remains to the Capital.

In the same article a moving tribute was paid to Baker Pasha.

It is not in military circles alone that the death of Valentine Baker will be heard of with sincere regret. Those who recall the error which deprived his Country of his services will remember also the terrible penalty he paid and the splendid atonement which he sought to make in the remnant of what at one time appeared a ruined career.

He was as a soldier one of the most dashing officers that the most brilliant department of the Service has ever produced.

No man has ever understood better the duties of a commander of cavalry, or fulfilled them with such general applause.

As a scholar and an explorer he was hardly less distinguished than by his courage in the field, and his sagacity in the councils of the camp.

He combined with the verve and pluck of Skebeleff, the patient political acumen of Napier.

The service he did in revealing to his countrymen the data of the Central Asian question has been attested by all who have followed him later in the same delicate field.

But the portion of his life which has passed since he ceased to bear Her Majesty's Commission is even richer in wholesome lessons. An ordinary spirit would have been broken by the severe penalties he had incurred. But Baker was not of the common mode.

Since he could no longer serve England, he set himself to serve English interests. The Sultan found him an indispensable adviser in a time of grave danger, and, when the misfortunes of Egypt appeared to have culminated, he hurried to undertake, in the face of the most discouraging surroundings, a post full of arduous responsibility.

In what spirit of self-sacrifice he set himself to discipline and encourage the dejected and broken soldiers of the Khedive the records, half melancholy, half glorious, of Tokar and Tamar show. For the moment, it appeared that even his gallant spirit and unceasing energy failed to restore the shattered fortune of the Egyptian armies; but if, to-day, the Khedive can rely with confidence upon the steadiness of his battalions as a buttress against invasion from the once-dreaded South, it is to Baker, and to Baker alone, that much of the fabric is due.

As organiser of the gendarmerie he displayed capacities for civil adminis-tration of no mean order.

There is something extremely pathetic in the obscure and gloomy close to what at one time promised to be a career of singular lustre. The favourite of society, the dashing cavalry officer, the lion of so many a gay coterie, has died far away from friends and home, and it is in a foreign land that his old comrades pay the last honours to his name.

The leading article ends with these words:

The Commander-in-Chief despatched instructions yesterday to Cairo, to the effect that the British troops in the garrison there are to pay all military honour to the late Colonel Valentine Baker. . . . It is needless to add that the sad event has cast a universal gloom over Cairo, where mourning is almost more for the loss of a private friend that for a public officer whose place it will be hard to fill.

Only two days after the sad news had been received in England, the Queen, who was at Balmoral, and had heard nothing, was enquiring of Lord Ponsonby why she had not heard any more of Valentine Baker's re-instatement. He informed her, sadly, of Valentine's death.

The account of the funeral itself was given in the *Standard* on 19 November:

The mortal remains of Baker Pasha were brought to Cairo late last night by train, and were at once taken to the house of General Stephenson.

The Duke of Cambridge telegraphed to General Stephenson to pay all honours due to so distinguished and brilliant a soldier, and those instruc-tions were carried out to the letter.

The funeral was fixed for three o'clock in the afternoon, long before which time a great crowd had assembled outside General Stephenson's house, whilst the procession, in the order indicated in my telegram of yes-terday, was being formed. When completed, it covered nearly three quarters of a mile.

On the way to the cemetery, the coffin, covered by a Union Jack, rested on a gun carriage. It was immediately followed by Captain Fortescue, carrying the medals and decorations of the deceased soldier on a velvet cushion.

Behind him was led Baker's favourite white charger. The pall-bearers were Generals Stephenson, Clery and Grenfell; Coe, Charles Baker, Lord Dunmore and Coles Pasha. The Khedive was represented by all his Aides-de-Camp and the Master of the Ceremonies.

The whole of the Ministry were present, as well as all officers of the

Egyptian Army, of the Police, and of the British Army in Egypt, together with the entire English Colony and a large number of foreigners.

Owing to the great length of the procession, the actual burial did not take place till nearly 5 o'clock. As the coffin, covered with wreaths, was lowered into the grave a hundred men fired three volleys over it, whilst an Egyptian battery outside the cemetery gave a salute of twelve guns.

It was pleasing to notice how thoroughly representative was the character of the attendance at the Funeral. Hardly a single familiar face was missing.
The universal esteem gained by Baker could scarcely have been better exemplified than by the kindly obituary notice which appeared in the 'Bosphorus Egyptian', this evening. It is needless to expiate on the general sorrow felt by the whole British Colony here.

This tribute was followed by a letter from Sir Evelyn Baring to the Marquess of Salisbury. (A copy of this letter is in the author's possession.)

Cairo
November 18th 1887

My Lord,

I had the honour to report to your Lordship in my telegram N. 251 of 17th inst. the sad and unexpected death of Valentine Baker Pasha, but I think it may not be out of place to add a few remarks on one who has held so prominent a position in Egypt during the last few years.

Baker Pasha was appointed to command the Gendarmerie and Police at a time when the restoration of public tranquillity and the formation of an efficient body of police was of paramount importance. Out of the materials at his command Baker Pasha organised a force which for the last five years has carried out the difficult task of preserving order both in the towns and provinces in a most satisfactory manner.

The immunities conferred upon foreign residents rendered this work more than usually delicate, but Baker Pasha, by the exercise of untiring care and tact succeeded in avoiding the dangers threatened by this somewhat difficult position.

Popular with his own men, and with the community in general, no one knew better than he how to develop the best qualities of his own Officers and no one was served with greater fidelity.

The Khedive and the Egyptian Government will feel the loss of this distinguished officer very severely. For my own part I have, I may say, been in almost daily communication with General Baker since my arrival in this Country. Greatly as I feel the personal loss, I consider the public loss both to myself and to the English Government as a still greater one.

The benefits General Baker has conferred upon Egypt, irrespective of his distinguished services elsewhere, are, of themselves, sufficient to show that by his death a man has been lost upon whose courage, ability and judgement not only England but the country which he was serving at the time of his death could confidently rely in the hour of need.

I have, etc. E. Baring

The Prime Minister, Lord Salisbury, replied:

5th December 1877

Sir,

The announcement of the death of General Valentine Baker Pasha, conveyed in your telegram of the 17th ultimo, was received by Her Majesty's Government with great regret. They were well aware of the important services which the deceased had rendered to the Egyptian Government since his appointment to command of the Gendarmerie and Police and they felt that the Khedive had lost in him a most valuable servant.

It is a satisfaction to me to be able to place on record my entire concurrence in the opinions which you express in your despatch Number 532 of the 18th Ultimo as to the importance and the difficulties of the task which was entrusted to Baker Pasha, the high qualities which he showed in surmounting these difficulties and the devotion and fidelity with which the duties of his office were performed.

I am, etc. Salisbury

Meanwhile Sir Samuel had obviously written to Sir Evelyn Baring on hearing the sad news, for Sir Evelyn replied privately:

Cairo
December 9th 1887

My dear Sir Samuel,

Our letters crossed. I did not write to you any of the details connected with your brother's death as I thought you would hear them from one of your daughters, who, allow me to say, behaved most nobly and pluckily under terribly distressing circumstances. For 24 hours they were quite alone without anyone to help them.

Miss Sybil Baker is still here, and, I think, intends to stay on for a short time. I need hardly say that if my wife and I can be of the smallest service to her we shall be only too pleased to do anything to help.

I miss your Brother more and more every day.

Believe me,
Yours sincerely,
Evelyn Baring.

But perhaps the saddest letter was written by his sister who ended her letter:

> Dear Val was laid very near his darling Hermione, just the other side of the path, with all possible military honours of a British General, which he would have been, had he lived a few *days* longer! It is all heartbreaking – but he rests at last – no one can hurt him any more.
>
> Dr Sandwich says that a year ago there were obscure symptoms of heart disease – or rather, I fancy a worn-out heart, – one may almost say literally a broken heart, broken by many sorrows, he told me so himself . . .

In another letter she adds:

> The dear Prince (of Wales) sympathises deeply, and I am overwhelmed with letters from all parts.

★ ★ ★

The traveller in Egypt in 1982, just ninety-five years after the death of General Valentine Baker, might still see the tablet, erected to him in the beautiful Cathedral, in Cairo, which owing to plans for a new bridge over the Nile, may soon be pulled down. The tablet reads:

In Memory of
Lieutenant General Valentine Baker Pasha who
died in Egypt Nov. 17th 1887
When in the Service of HH the Khedive
as Inspector General of the Egyptian Constabulary.
He commanded for many years HM 10th Royal Hussars
and subsequently entered the service of
HTM The Sultan of Turkey
In which he obtained the rank of Lieutenant General.
He highly distinguished himself at the battle of
Tashkessan when in command of a small Turkish Force
covering the retreat of the Sultan's troops in their
attempt to relieve Plevna, a service which was
brilliantly and successfully carried out by him in
face of a considerably superior force of the enemy.
This tablet is erected by his numerous sincere friends
and admirers as a token of their respect
and appreciation of qualities of the highest order
which he possessed as a
soldier and commander.

A copy of these words, written in the hand of General Sir Frederick Stephenson and dated May, 1889, is still treasured in the Baker family.

And so a gallant soldier was laid to rest far from home.

It was tragic that he did not know, when he died, of his Queen's forgiveness. For so many years he had fulfilled his promise of serving Her interests in exile, and, although he must have known of the appreciation felt for him by the Prince of Wales, it was the final forgiveness and his re-instatement in the British Army that were denied him by only a few days.

In the quiet cemetery in Cairo, where he is laid to rest, the hot tropical sun beats down at mid-day, but in the cool of the evening as the grey leaves of the Eucalyptus trees rustle gently over them, and the shadows lengthen, the graves of General Valentine Baker and Hermione, his beautiful golden-haired daughter, lie peacefully side by side. To those travellers visiting them, it may all seem so very long ago, but under that grey stone there lies a gallant and faithful, if broken heart.

INDEX

Note: SB = (Sir) Samuel Baker; VB = Valentine Baker

178